KU-735-901

What Are You Looking At?

Queer Sex, Style and Cinema

Paul Burston

CASSELL

Cassell
Wellington House
London
WC2R 0BB

215 Park Avenue South
New York
NY 10003

© Paul Burston 1995

All rights reserved. No part of this publication may be
reproduced or transmitted in any form or by any means,
electronic or mechanical including photocopying, recording
or any information storage or retrieval system, without
prior permission in writing from the publishers.

First published 1995

British Library Cataloguing-in-Publication Data
A catalogue record for this book is available from the
British Library.

ISBN: 0-304-34300-5

Typeset by York House Typographic Ltd, London
Printed and bound in Great Britain by Mackays of Chatham plc

Cover photographs by Robert Taylor
Cover design by Jamie Janner

What Are You Lookin. ...?

DISCARD

BATH SPA UNIVERSITY
LIBRARY

B.C.H.E. – LIBRARY

00069456

The Cassell Lesbian and Gay Studies list offers a broad-based platform to lesbian, gay and bisexual writers for the discussion of contemporary issues and for the promotion of new ideas and research.

COMMISSIONING:
Steve Cook

CONSULTANTS:
Liz Gibbs
Keith Howes (Austrailia)
Christina Ruse
Peter Tatchell

BATH COLLEGE OF HIGHER EDUCATION
DISCARD 301.424
SOMERSET PLACE
BATH BA1 5HB   BUR

Contents

4   *Cinema*

5   *Symptoms*

Foreword

WHAT'S a nice girl like me doing in a queer place like this? Well, since you ask, I had better declare my interests, both personal and political. I have known Paul Burston for some time now, since he mugged me at a party a few years ago. Part pushy bastard with a head full of awkward questions and a pocketful of poppers, part slave to the rhythm – we were bound to get on. Politically, it's different. He is a gay man and I am not. While I often write about sexual politics, I tend to find the debates of the gay press too insular, too inward-looking for my liking. I guess that's why I like Paul's work, because it refuses to be happening within the feminist arena, where feminism has become so academically rarefied that it has lost contact with any political base whatsoever or where it has been simplified into dull essentialism.

The articles in this book are pitched somewhere between academia and activism. The space they occupy is that of popular journalism, and this, of course, is a place I have a lot of time for. To engage with popular culture from within popular culture is the best job in the world and the easiest to get wrong. To be critical of the things you love, to be sparky, to be a fan, to be an *agent provacateur*, to represent your own political position, to represent everyone else's and at the end of the day to write something that entertains people enough to make them read it to the end ain't as easy as it looks.

The title of this collection – *What Are You Looking At?* – signals an aggressive rather than a defensive stance and that I think is typical of the new generation of queer writers. Straight culture likes to kid itself that it can cream off the best of gay culture without having to deal with gay people themselves. As soon as gay people start demanding anything nearing equality they are accused of being too 'in your face'. *What Are You Looking At?* is unashamedly in your face. There are no apologies here. 'Just what is your problem?' is the question that Burston is continually asking of straight society.

But if he is hard on us heterosexuals, even 'gay-acting' ones, he is equally hard on those he is seen to represent. I had better warn you now that if you are a happy homosexual, all snuggled up in the welcoming biceps of the 'gay community', then I'm not sure how much you'll like this book. If you are a tolerant heterosexual who thinks gays are fine just so long as they don't interfere with you, then you won't like it either. And if you think you already know where you stand on issues from gay porn to laughing jokes about AIDS, then I can guarantee you'll positively hate it. If on the other hand, you like your cultural politics with ice and a slice, shaken and stirred, you might just knock this back in one hit. This collection of essays is that most lethal kind of cocktail. Don't be fooled by the little umbrellas, the deception fizz and the gorgeous colours – this one packs a punch. While you're reeling, you will find out that the problem with gay porn according to Burston is that it's not gay enough, that taking E every weekend is fine but don't try claiming hedonism as a political act. Even being gay is not good 'when it is used to bankroll mediocrity'. Sometimes I think, 'He only does it annoy, because he knows it teases'. (Then, naturally, I take him aside and talk harshly to him before I beat him.) Other times I think he does it because he likes a ruck. Mostly, I have to say I think he does it because be is an impatient bugger. If he is critical of what a gay identity has come to mean in the 1990s, he is not afraid to turn that critical awareness on himself. Hence he is prepared to venture into those areas that unsettle us all, whether gay or straight. Thus with supreme contrariness he admits to being turned on not just by photos of women, but of oh-my-god lesbians. He puts himself on the line when he discusses photographer Della Grace's work and (literally) when he takes his clothes off for her. His tattoos were meant to be deep and meaningful but he realizes that they are marks of superficiality. While enjoying Tom Kalin's stylish movie *Swoon*, Burston's discomfort at the glamorization of its horrific murder is pronounced.

This continual skating between image and some much bigger reality is there too in his interviews with various pop stars. Burston is clearly interested in questions of accountability, about what it means to be an openly gay icon, but never in a straightforward way. He can't help but be fascinated by ambiguity, recognizing that what matters is not whether Keanu or Take That are really gay but the wider cultural implications of their slippery representations. He is fundamentally interested in the pose as well as the politics of gay culture.

In the last section of the book, 'Symptoms', where he looks at issues surrounding the portrayal of AIDS, he finds responses to the epidemic cropping up in the most unlikely places, from Cronenberg films to disco music. Once more Burston is concerned not so much with what is politically correct but with what is actually political. Here his anger is at its most tangible, but there is optimism in his anger. In the collective mourning for lost times and lost friends that he feels on the dance floor, he also sees a strategy for survival.

The dance floor is not a bad place to end up, I guess. After all, no one can read Judith Butler all night long, and so that is where you will usually find him should you need to take issue with any of his opinions. If you can pin the disco bunny down, you will be able to participate in a frank exchange of views. You may not like what he says, you may think that on the dance floor no one can hear you scream but then you haven't met Paul. He can shout louder over the music than anyone I know. This is his real talent. The fact that he can do it in more ways than one is what makes him worth listening to.

Suzanne Moore

Preface

I NEVER wanted to be a gay journalist. Don't get me wrong. The thought of performing obscene physical acts with another man appealed to me long before I summoned the courage to go out and find a man prepared to act the part. Similarly, the thought of being paid to mouth off about the things I care about struck me as a very nice idea, long before I realized I could make a comfortable living out of it. I just never imagined there might be a convenient way of combining the two.

There are times when I'm still not sure there is. While I am, for the most part, glad to be called gay, and regard journalism, along with prostitution, as one of the least understood, most noble professions open to a young man of sound mind and firm body, there are occasions when 'gay' and 'journalist' don't make particularly good bedfellows.

One of the first lessons you learn as a critic is that nobody questions your right to express an opinion when it happens to match their own. It's only when you dare to say something they disagree with that rights are challenged and knives drawn. When you're seen – rightly or (more often) wrongly – to represent a section of the population who aren't used to seeing their views expressed in print, things can get rather bloody. I once received a letter from a fellow gay hack, advising me that, given my profile (I take it he wasn't referring to my strong jaw and noble nose), I had certain 'responsibilities' – responsibilities which should, as he put it, 'weigh heavy'.

What he really meant to say, of course, was that I was perfectly entitled to an opinion, just so long as it was the opinion of that diverse group of people collectively known as the 'gay community'. I think it should go without saying that anyone who claims to speak on behalf of a bunch of people who rarely agree about anything should be treated with the utmost caution. To even consider making such a ridiculous declaration has always struck me as the height of impertinence. Besides which, it has very little to do with journalism. If anyone wants to know what the gay community thinks about a particular subject, I suggest they commission a market research study.

There are days when I would sooner write about anything but the latest gay film, fashion accessory, pop personality or political performance. There is only so much you can say about the costs of representing ourselves, or the value of Madonna's latest tourist trip, and when saying anything at all opens you to charges of letting the side down it can get a little wearying. So why do I do it?

I do it because, on a good day, the thrill I get out of putting proper words in improper places exceeds the excitement of even that first homosexual encounter. I do it because there are still some things worth writing about, and because writing about them from my singular perspective has been known to result in a bulging mailbag and a queer quotation on Page Three of *The Sun* (my love-letter to Superman, included in this volume, was squeezed next to the boobs in Britain's best-selling tabloid). I do it because nothing irritates the homophobes in the British media quite so much as a gay man with a big mouth and a byline. But mostly I do it because, as yet, I haven't found a more rewarding way of showing off.

Finally, a word about the title. *What Are You Looking At?* was my boyfriend's idea. I stuck with it – partly because my editor was breathing down my neck and, try as I might, I couldn't think of anything snappier in the short time before his catalogue went to print, partly because, on reflection, it seemed to sum up the contents of the book, reflecting my unnatural obsession with the ways gay men look at themselves, each other and the culture around them.

Plus, of course, it conveys the right measure of attitude.

Paul Burston
London, June 1995

Acknowledgements

SOME of the articles in this book have been published (usually in very different, shorter, forms) in the following publications:

Attitude	'My Own Private Keanu'; 'The Boy Who Came Back'; 'Oh, Donna'; 'Neil Tennant, Honestly" 'Gay Acting'
Capital Gay	'Putting My Foot in It'
City Limits	'Jason Talks Straight'
Gay Times	'I'll Grumble for Ya'; 'Demolition Men'; 'Sound and Vision'
ID	'Ring My Bell'
The Independent	'Bigmouth Strikes Again'; 'Life's a Drag'
The Modern Review	'Rescue Me'; 'Masculinity: Complex?'
Time Out	'Sex on the Brain'; 'Boys Keep Swinging'; 'Richard Loves Cindy'; 'Singing Lessons'; 'Drug Queens'; 'Brawn in the USA'; 'Hetero Hell'; 'End of the Road'; 'Genre Bender'; 'Cruising the Vampire'; 'Seeing the Funny Side'

The author and publisher wish to thank Faber and Faber for permission to reprint lines from the following copyright material on pages 151 and 155:

Sylvia Plath, 'Lady Lazarus, from *Ariel*.

And thanks

Even know-it-alls need a little help from their friends.

Thanks to Jeremy Clarke, Steve Cook, Susannah Frankel, Lorraine Gamman, Andrew Loxton, Carl Miller, Deborah Orr, Gordon Rainsford, Andrew Tuck, Johnny Volcano, Tom Wakefield.

Special thanks to Mark Simpson, who keeps my green light flashing, and to the late Spud Jones, who never stopped kicking against the pricks.

This book is dedicated to him, and to my boyfriend, William, who got me through it.

Part one

Sex

Homosexual Acts

THERE are no gay men in commercial gay porn films. There are men who suck cock; men who instruct other men on how to suck cock; men who say things like 'yeah, tighten that ass'; and men who take it up the bum while bending over leatherette sofas and knocking their heads against potted palms. There are men who wake up feeling horny in shared prison cells; men who get erections standing around in communal showers; men whose girlfriends simply aren't giving them enough; men who complain about the need to shoot their load; and men who turn to their best buddy whenever they need a helping hand, tongue or pound of gristle. But there are no – repeat no – men who are actually, y'know, *gay* or anything.

Okay, so I'm exaggerating. Grab yourself a stack of gay porn videos, spend an afternoon with your finger firmly on the fast-forward button, and the chances are you will come across a few scenes in which nobody claims to be 'just foolin' around', nobody mentions their 'girlfriend' and nobody refers to anybody as a 'dirty faggot'. If you're really lucky, you might even lay hands on a Jeff Stryker video in which the world's most celebrated 'asexual' porn star has a boyfriend – straight-acting, of course.

But these are still the exceptions to the rule. One of the most interesting contradictions of gay porn is that, while gay men celebrate it as one of the few forms of representation in which homosexual acts are revealed in terms that are both explicit and clearly pleasurable, it is also one in which homosexuality itself tends to be screened out of the picture. In her review of Jerry Douglas's award-winning 'gay porn cruises gay politics' feature *More of a Man* (1990), Mandy Merck refers to gay porn's 'crucial affirmation of homosexual identity'.[1] But *More of a Man*, if not entirely unique, is certainly unusual in its effort to relate the pleasures of sex to the politics of coming out. Rarely do the men in gay porn films identify themselves as gay. In the overwhelming majority of porn scenarios, homosexual sex is represented as the unavoidable consequence of two or more men being thrown together into a sexually frustrating situation, rather than an expression of active homosexual desire. Hence the choice of settings: prison cells, locker rooms, military academies – anywhere, in fact, where the absence of women can be explained in such a way as to avoid raising any doubts about the sexuality of the men engaged in what are very obviously homosexual practices. As Mark Simpson rightly points out, 'almost never is the situation a recognizably gay one: men are hardly ever picked up in gay bars or bath-houses'.[2]

It is this question of recognition, of the 'realness' of gay porn that I want to consider here. I realize, of course, that 'reality' is not a quality we normally associate with porn, gay or otherwise. As every sucker knows, porn is all about fantasy: it isn't supposed to be 'real'. In a sense, this is absolutely true. Gay porn films are 'all about fantasy' – or, more precisely, they are a physical record of one, two or more men acting out a sexual fantasy for the sexual gratification of those watching at home (or, in more enlightened countries than Britain, at the local porn cinema). Moreover, many gay porn films are, literally, 'about' fantasy, in as much as they incorporate elements of sexual fantasy into their narrative structure, thereby drawing attention to the phantasmagoric function of porn as a whole.

To take a recent example, two out of the four scenarios in *Command Performance* (1992) are clearly staged as sexual fantasies. In the first, a customer at a piano repair shop imagines himself having sex with the hunky repair boy. In the second, a member of the audience at a piano recital visualizes himself screwing the pianist. This scene is even (artificially) timed to climax in time with the audience's applause. The goatee beards, Calvin Klein underwear and disclaimers about the role of fantasy and the representation of safer sexual practices date this as very much a 1990s film. Otherwise, there is nothing especially new or unusual about *Command Performance*. Elements of sexual fantasy also provide narrative drive in *A Matter of Size* (1984), *Something Wild* (1984) and *Behind Closed Doors* (1989). The episodic, anti-realist structure of films like these, together with the emphasis on sex-as-performance in titles such as *Screen Play* (1984) and *Delusion* (1992), all support Richard Dyer's recent observation that 'gay film/video porn has consistently been marked by self-reflexivity, by texts that have wanted to draw attention to themselves as porn, that is, as constructed presentations of sex'.[3]

At the same time, gay porn strives for a certain degree of 'realness' – and by this I don't only mean the notion of 'real' (i.e., 'straight') masculinity discussed by Simpson. As Merck points out, 'porn movies traditionally offer one claim to realism – the actual performance of intercourse in the pro-filmic event'.[4] How convincing does this performance of sex have to be seen to be, in order to arouse the viewer effectively and achieve what Dyer neatly refers to as 'its orgasmic aim'? This is the question foremost in the minds of the industry's commercial producers and directors. Operating in a culture where gay sexual activity is still (for the most part) censored out of existence or distorted out of recognition, the makers of gay porn go to all kinds of lengths to persuade us that what we are watching is 'real' sex – in spite of our knowledge that everything we are seeing has been carefully lit, timed, staged and edited. Hence the wide variety of camera angles, the tight close-ups on genitals, the extra lighting to illuminate fully the point of penetration – all conspiring to show us (as both Dyer and Simpson have remarked) more than we could ever hope to see during the experience of actually having sex ourselves.

If the sex depicted in commercial gay porn films seems at times to be verging more on the hyper-real than the merely real, at no point is this more obvious than in the event that is commonly known as the 'cum-shot'. And it is an 'event' – the intense build-up of music and sense of pure visual spectacle leaves us in no doubt about that. Even before AIDS, the men in gay porn adhered to the directive 'on me, not in me'. Ironically, it is concerns about 'realness', rather than safety, which still prompt a porn star to withdraw at the point of orgasm. Often shown in slow-motion, sometimes repeated for extra emphasis, the 'cum-shot' is intended to be read as a measure of the pleasure, and the 'reality', of what we have just witnessed – the final, irrefutable proof that 'real' sex did take place. The irony, of course, is that the technical tailoring of the 'cum-shot' effectively robs the scene of any realism it might have held. Or, to put it another way, we all know perfectly well that nobody 'cums' dressed quite like that.

The tension between the need to persuade us that what we are seeing is 'real' (i.e., recognizable) and the urge to titillate us with images that are the stuff of pure fantasy (i.e., most desirable) lies at the heart of commercial gay porn. In his review of the year's heart-throbs and throbbing members, *The Best of the Superstars 1994: The Year in Sex*, John Patrick notes that 'gay men get from porn what they can't get otherwise'.[5] Apart from drawing us towards the uncharitable conclusion that the men who watch gay porn films are a sad and lonely bunch of wankers, his observation invites us to consider what, exactly, it is that we might get from porn that we can't get from sex. One obvious answer is: a partner who never says no, who never has a headache, who is willing and able to keep going all night long. It is one of the main selling points of gay porn that it is able to offer us 'more' of what we desire: more men, more sex, more inches, more orgasms that it ever seemed possible to pack into ninety minutes. The titles make the boasts explicit: *Sex Bazaar, Ultimate Desires, Like A Horse, Superhunks, Loaded, Powertool, Inch by Inch, The Bigger the Better*.

Only sometimes more is less, and this is so often the case with a form of entertainment in which nothing is left to the imagination, in which everything is overstated, overloaded and overburdened with the ambition to arouse an immediate erotic response. Excess isn't always the surest means to success, and while there may be some considerable truth in the notion that the harder they come, the harder they'll sell, gay porn's appetite for over-developed bodies and under-developed characters and plots can leave an audience hungering after a bit of reality.

On top of which, the urge to 'pack it all in' (and thereby give us more of 'what we want') can – and often does – result in work which is formulaic and banal. Chet Thomas, house director at Catalina (one of the largest American producers of gay porn films and videos) describes the demands of his job thus: 'I have three minutes for sucking in this position, three minutes for that position, two minutes for dialogue, two minutes for dildos or rimming or some other action, three minutes for the first fuck position, three minutes for the second fuck position, a half minute for cum-shots and a minute for dialogue and fade out. It all comes down to mathematics.' Reducing sex to the rules of arithmetic is one way of taking all the joy out of it. After all, it is the element of surprise, of spontaneity that contributes to the pleasure we experience when having sex. Clumsiness isn't always such a bad thing either. One of the most frequent complaints made about commercial gay porn is that it is too rehearsed, too polished, too perfect to be truly sexy – by which people usually mean, it isn't 'real' enough to be 'useful'.

Nowadays, the 'usefulness' of porn is something people tend to talk about whenever the subject of explicit sexual representation rears its head. We hear that porn is 'useful' because it provides a safe alternative to sexual contact, because it demonstrates the erotic potential of safer sexual practices, because it vitally affirms the pleasures of gay sex at a time when all else is preaching doom and gloom. It is this notion of porn's 'usefulness' which was instrumental in bringing gay porn out of the closet and onto the shelves, in the shape of all the gay sex education videos you can now buy over the counter at a number of highstreet outlets throughout Britain. What is especially interesting about these videos is the way in which they attempt to replicate the aesthetic excesses of hardcore gay porn while taking care to observe the specific demands placed on them – both as educational resources, and as licensed depictions of practices widely held to be 'pornographic' by their very nature.

The British gay sex video boom began in June 1992, with the launch of *The Gay Man's Guide to Safer Sex*. Backed by the Terrence Higgins Trust, and granted an 18 certificate by the British Board of Film Classification, *The Gay Man's Guide* wears its 'usefulness' like a talisman against criticism. In the week of its release, the Trust even issued a press statement claiming 'this isn't pornography, it's an erotic lifesaver'. There is a certain degree of truth in this. On the one hand, the combination of five frankly horny scenarios and snippets of professional advice offered in the video does make a lot more educational sense than a load of old icebergs.

On the other hand, both the tone and (to a certain degree) the sexual content of the video are undeniably pornographic. The lighting, camera angles, and music score all echo gay porn's strange grip on 'reality'. The video even features a 'real' gay porn star (Aiden Shaw, who appears in *Command Performance* and a number of other titles for Catalina). All that's really missing is that final token of 'realism', the 'cum-shot'.

In a somewhat defensive press statement issued to journalists along with preview copies of the video, the promoters laboured the point that 'sex is not a rational activity', insisting that 'erotic images of safer sex can dispel ideas that it is unfulfilling or boring', that 'explicit images of gay sexuality are common currency in the gay media' and that 'anything too sanitised or coy would inevitably lack impact'. In many respects, the decision not to shy away from explicit sexual representation was a commendable one. Certainly there is little evidence to suggest that sanitized images of sexuality have the effect of persuading anyone, least of all gay men, to alter their sexual behaviour. Nor does it seem very likely that a few soft-focus shots of half-dressed men would have taken *The Gay Man's Guide* straight to the top of Virgin's in-store video chart.

But whatever the strengths of its commercial performance, or merits as an educational resource, in its attempt to impart information about safer sex via the 'common currency' of porn *The Gay Man's Guide* inevitably sets up a tension between what it says it wants to show us – i.e., real gay men enjoying (safer) sex – and what it actually does show us – i.e., real gay men acting as though they were porn stars, pretending to enjoy simulated sex. Perhaps gay men really do all fancy themselves as porn stars, and will happily adopt any behavioural patterns they think might make them more like their idols – even if that means adjusting to sexual practices they previously regarded as 'unfulfilling' or 'boring'. Whatever the reasoning behind *The Gay Man's Guide*, the net effect is of a video that looks as though it would dearly like to be a porn film when it grows up.

Indeed, the same could be said of most of the gay sex education/erotic entertainment videos now weighing down the shelves. The titles (*Getting It Right*, *Better Gay Sex*, *Power and Grace*, *Love Muscles*, *Overload*) echo gay porn's obsession with achieving 'more better sex now'. The videos themselves are intent on showing us less – less explicit sex, less visual excitement, even less proof of 'reality'. This wouldn't matter quite so much were it not for the fact that, with very few exceptions, these videos are as boring and formulaic as the very worst gay porn. Packed with 'crucial', 'sensational' 'guys', they each try to compensate for their lack of orgasmic achievement with regular overdoses of arty freeze-frame photography and pounding techno backing tracks. Pump without action, gloss without sex, the best one can say about them is that they look like Bananarama videos with Bananarama taken out.

If it's sex without gloss you want, you have to look to the margins, to the growing number of home-recorded porn titles. Shot on camcorders with little or no thought for sound, lighting or artistry, most are badly filmed and barely edited, with 'actors' who have a habit of giggling in the middle of their sexual 'performances' and 'directors' who can usually be heard mumbling instructions from behind the camera. Unpolished, unskilled and often clumsy, these videos are as close to the experience of having sex that you can get, which inevitably means that they are often filled with disappointments, but also means that you may see a few things – or even people – you recognize.

Notes

1. Mandy Merck, 'More of a Man', in *Perversions* (Virago Press, 1993), p. 217.
2. Mark Simpson, 'A World of Penises', in *Male Impersonators* (Cassell, 1994), p. 133.
3. Richard Dyer, 'Idol Thoughts', *Critically Queer; Critical Quarterly*, **36** (1) (Spring 1994), p. 54.
4. Merck, p. 224.
5. John Patrick, *The Best of the Superstars 1994: The Year in Sex* (Starbooks Press, 1994), p. 493.

Putting My Foot in It

I WANT to write about how I'm turned on by a photograph in a book published by Gay Men's Press. The photograph shows two figures dressed in leather, adorned with all the usual paraphernalia of an SM fantasy – harnesses, dog-collars, studs and chains. The one kneeling has cropped hair and a heavy torso embellished with tattoos. The one standing has powerful thighs and black rubber gloves reaching up to the elbows. The erotic signifiers of this scenario wouldn't be out of place in a photograph by Mapplethorpe or a drawing by Tom of Finland. Like many gay men, the construction of my sexual identity has been conditioned to varying degrees by the output of both artists. The difference here is that the photographer and the models acting out the fantasy aren't men at all, but lesbians. The book is called *Love Bites* (GMP, 1992). The photographer is called Della Grace. I want to write about how I'm turned on by this photograph, but I'm wondering whether I even have the right, and assuming I do, whether anyone is willing to listen.

The relationship between lesbian sex and gay male sexuality is something we are not supposed to talk about. It is, or so we are told, a dirty secret, and a politically dangerous one. For all our supposed awareness of the dangers of a closet mentality, sometimes it seems as though our oppressors have taught us alarmingly well. When lesbian journalist Cherry Smyth asked, during a conference on Queer at the London Institute of Contemporary Arts in 1992, whether gay men perceived lesbian sex as unphallic and boring, or were simply afraid of putting the proverbial foot in it, she provoked an embarrassed silence.

Through her photography, Della Grace has dared not only to question the relationship between lesbian and gay sexual practice but actually to bring it into view. The women in her photographs revel in the traditional iconography of gay male sex; they perform fellatio on dildos; they harness one another into positions of dominance and submission. It's a far cry from the strictly-no-penetration, psychic lesbian sexuality advocated by separatists, or the soft-focus lesbian foreplay found in straight porn scenarios.

No wonder, then, that the silence has been deafening. Not one of the women's publishing houses would touch Grace's work.

The sisters at Sisterwrite bookshop refused to stock it, the implication being that Della had betrayed lesbian political consciousness, had fallen from grace. 'My images are political', she asserts in her defence. 'My purpose is to provide positive images of my sexuality and the sexuality of the women I idenfity with, who are part of a community that is considered "politically incorrect". SM dykes have been ostracised, labelled "fascists" or "pseudo-men". The women I photograph are women who want to express who they are. In Britain especially, lesbian sexuality is so invisible. I want women who see my book to recognise that they're okay, that there's nothing wrong with them.'

The invisibility of lesbian sexuality is symptomatic of a culture organized around the notion of the phallus as *the* symbol of desire. (Gay men have an easier time of it. After all, there's not a lot we don't know about cock worship.) More so than gay male sex – of which there are some, albeit problematic, widely-recognized images – lesbian sex is largely unimaginable to the general population, to whom notions of sexual activity are reducible to a preoccupation with finding out where the dick fits. A number of lesbian commentators have observed that, in trying to find means of representing what to many people is unrepresentable, lesbian artists have been obliged to appropriate dominant, phallocentric images of sexuality.

Writing in the now-defunct lesbian and gay quarterly *Out/ Look*, Julia Creet identified 'the phallic economy of the structures surrounding the production of lesbian sexual images' and argued the case for lesbians broadening their sexual knowledge and techniques through alliances with gay men. 'Why not look to gay men?' she asked. 'Our brothers have created institutions out of fantasies, while we lesbians are still arguing over whether to engage in fantasy in the first place.' Pat Califia revealed to *The Advocate* as early as 1983 that gay male friends and lovers had taught her things she would never have learned within the lesbian community. Lesbian friends of mine tell me they've been getting off on gay porn films for years.

If the coming together of lesbians and gay men in response to AIDS and the attacks of the Far Righteous is helping to dismantle the prejudice surrounding such 'confessions', it isn't happening nearly fast enough for Della Grace, who is tired of being made the scapegoat for other people's hang-ups. 'I didn't become a lesbian in order to have rules imposed on me', she protests. 'Gender-play is curious. It's been okay for years for gay men to play at being women, or for one partner to act the part, but for women to indulge in gender-fuck somehow isn't acceptable. But lesbians do. Lesbians even have gay male sex.'

One of the photographs in her 'Ruff Sex' sequence shows a woman being fucked from behind with a dildo in what could easily be read as a gay rape fantasy. Grace is perfectly happy for men, gay or straight, to derive erotic stimulation from such images ('so long as they don't do it in my face'), but resists the suggestion that the iconography and dynamics she employs are specifically male, classing them instead as 'butch' or 'fetish'. Her distinction is helpful if we are to make sense of the fact that her work does allow for multiple readings. 'Butch' elicits an erotic response across boundaries of gender and sexuality. Contrary to offering a simple re-enactment of fixed gender roles (as some critics have alleged), Grace's photographs provide a complex exploration of the categories 'male' and 'female'. Ultimately, a photograph of a lesbian wearing a dildo invites a different set of responses than one of a man brandishing an erection. Creet suggests that lesbian 'maleness' in this context may be a version of 'gay maleness'. But, as Grace points out, gay male sexual influence is only a part of what comprises her representation of what is, after all, lesbian sex.

So how am I (how are we?) to make sense of my (our?) erotic response? I wouldn't be the first gay man ever to fantasize about (or actually have) sex with women, but when we're dealing with *lesbian* images of *lesbian* women the familiar debate around the political 'rights' and 'wrongs' of bisexuality takes on a whole new meaning, becomes laden with a further set of 'consequences'. When the second issue of *Rouge* magazine was launched with a cover-photograph by Grace reproduced as a promotional poster, a number of gay men I know ended up with an image on their wall of an androgynous-looking model with muscular thighs wearing Doc Martens and a tutu. At least two gay pubs in central London displayed the same poster alongside the usual array of boy-shots. When the third issue of the magazine appeared, and it was explained to those who'd mistaken the model for a pretty boy that she was in fact a lesbian, the posters inexplicably came down.

11: *Putting My Foot in It*

Yet if we are to accept that gay men have become fetishized sex-symbols in many lesbian erotic fantasies, indeed if we only acknowledge that the iconography and dynamics we commonly associate with gay male sexuality can be appropriated successfully by lesbians, we must also allow that images of lesbian sexuality can provide erotic stimulus for gay men. Could it be that the gender-bending traditions of both our communities, coupled with the disruption of gender-norms through parody (the masquerade of exaggerated masculinity, the fetish of extreme femininity), have led to the creation of a realm of erotic fantasy wherein sexual and gender boundaries can be crossed? Could we be talking about the possibility of a shared homoerotic space? After spending the last ten years 'coming together', could lesbians and gay men be on the verge of 'cumming' together? Perhaps it's high time we as gay men overcame our fear of 'putting our foot in it'. Given that lesbians like Grace have taken the lead in raising these concerns, surely it's simply a matter of putting the shoe on the other foot?

Sex on the Brain

MY mother made me a homosexual. At least that's what people tell me. Straight society's obsession with queerness has given rise to some pretty peculiar notions over the years, but none so persistant as the one claiming that a mother's love can bend a little boy's libido. Like John Stykes, the straight-talking film director in *Valley of the Dolls*, 'I'm tired of all these fancy doctors who blame everything on the poor mothers of this world.'

Besides, I'm far more inclined to attribute my sexual leanings to the fact that I was the last kid on our street to own an Action Man with gripping hands. And the first to discover that he had very little down there to get a grip on. And I do sometimes wonder whether I wouldn't have straightened out had I not gone through puberty so thoroughly tuned in to the sounds of the 1970s. Stepping into a pair of Cuban heels at the tender age of eleven couldn't have helped matters. By the time I was thirteen I could barely even walk straight. Blame it on the Bee Gees. Blame it on the boogie.

The in thing these days is to blame it on biology. First we had Simon LeVay telling us that homosexuality is all in the mind – or at least a small part of it known as the 'hypothalamus'. Then we were swamped with reports about a bunch of boffins who claimed to have discovered a 'gay gene', passed (as Lady Luck would have it) from mother to son. Well, not exactly. Despite speculation in the great British tabloids about the identification of a 'genetic disorder' providing just grounds for abortion, the plain fact of the matter is that the gene itself has yet to be located. What the scientists think they might have found is evidence linking a region of the X chromosome (which all male babies inherit from their mothers) with the sexual orientation of some gay men. Sixty-six gay men, to be precise.

What is clear is that the pursuit of a biological explanation for human sexuality is not an exact science. LeVay's claim that he had pinpointed a structural difference between the brains of homosexual and heterosexual men took little account of the fact that, while some of the gay men in his suspiciously small sample possessed a smaller hypothalamus than many of the straight men, some size queens boasted far larger ones. And what about bisexuals? Does their grey matter swell or shrink according to whom they're fucking, or does it weigh in midway between two averages?

Similarly, the facts behind the 'gay gene' theory beg a few questions. The study was led by Dr Dean Hamer, an AIDS researcher at the US National Cancer Institute. It began by delving into the family histories of 114 gay men, 13.5 per cent of whom were found to have a brother who was also gay. How much significance you attach to this statistic really depends on whether you trust recent surveys suggesting that lesbians, gay men and bisexuals of both sexes account for only 1 per cent of the general population. Given the public's capacity for telling porkies about all things remotely sexual, I'm inclined to think that a little scepticism wouldn't go amiss.

But it gets even better. Genetic tests were carried out on forty pairs of gay brothers. Of these, thirty-three pairs appeared to have inherited certain 'genetic markers'. Leaving aside the question of how these markers were conclusively linked to sexual activity, I do find myself worrying slightly about the remaining seven pairs of brothers. Were they lying when they said they were gay? Were they all like Brett Anderson of Suede – posing as sodomites whilst never having had a homosexual experience? Were their gay markers rubbed off during a teenage fumble with a big-breasted girl in the back seat of a Ford Cortina? I think we should be told.

I can't say I'm particularly thrilled at the thought of some strange man meddling with my genes – or my jeans for that matter. Unwelcome sexual advances I've learned to cope with – a sharp knee to the groin usually does the trick. Unwelcome scientific 'advances' are always a bit more complicated. A few days after the 'gay gene' fiasco made it on to the cover of practically every British newspaper, my mother phoned to chat idly about the weather. And to find out what I thought about 'this gay chromosome thing'.

I could tell straight off that mother wasn't quite herself today; I could hear the panic in her voice long distance. Her initial response when I came out to her was to ask in all seriousness whether I blamed her for making me gay – now it looked as though the buck was going to stop with her after all. I assured her that I thought the whole story was a load of old tosh, that I didn't believe something as complex as sexuality could be reduced to a few chromosomes, that in any case I didn't regard my sexuality as something I should 'blame' anyone for.

Finally, just to lighten her up a little, I told her that I could foresee some positive benefit, should some mad scientist ever prove the existence of a 'gay gene'. If homosexual babies could be identified in the womb, then it follows that heterosexual babies could be too. And just think of the benefits that might yield in light of the over-population problem: 'Sorry Missus, but it looks as if little Johnny is going to be a breeder after all, and I'm afraid we've got far too many of them cluttering up the planet already . . . '

Letting the Side Down

LATELY I've been experiencing a few problems with my erectile tissue. It all began when my friend Della asked me to pose for a series of photos intended for an exhibition on the theme of women looking at men. The exhibition was entitled 'What She Wants'. What she wanted was my dick. In the raw. Standing to attention. Responding to the loving caress of her lens.

Now I don't mind admitting I'm a bit of a show-off. If it was exhibition material she wanted, she'd come to the right man. Modesty aside, I regard myself as a model exhibitionist. Not in the textbook sense, you understand. I don't derive sexual pleasure from exposing myself to others in situations where such behaviour is clearly inappropriate. I never joined ranks with the boys who lined up to press their bare backsides against the rear window of the school bus. I don't run around the local park in a dirty raincoat, flashing my credentials at elderly women. I never (or very rarely) stand naked near the window with the lights on.

I just enjoy being photographed. Somewhere in leafy Hampstead there are a handful of Polaroids testifying to my one remotely irregular proclivity. Cameras turn me on. So much so that when Della made her unusual request my first thought was, why not? Given my peculiar penchant for all things photographic, I couldn't foresee there being any problem. I agreed.

I then spent the next three days telling myself why not. Because I ought to preserve a little mystery, that's why not. Because I'd put on a few pounds on holiday. Because I was bound to develop a pimple on my bum. Because people I neither knew nor cared about might see me exposed and laugh or, worse still, form some sort of pathological attachment to my naked image. Because I might never get laid in London again. Because boys who went on to higher education aren't supposed to do such things. What the hell, because my mother might find out!

This was Phase One. Phase Two involved equal measures of soul-searching and body-probing. I seem to spend half my life writing about sex, the other half talking about writing about it. Surely it was time I proved my commitment, gave it a bit less mouth and no trousers? Didn't I have a responsibility to experience the things I wrote about? On the other hand, would I measure up? Never mind maintaining professional standards, would I stand a chance of maintaining anything in full knowledge of how the competition fared on the inches scale? The men in gay porn movies (still one of the few media where you can be guaranteed of seeing a man in full flourish) all wield dicks the size of cucumbers. It's all part of the job, living up to the promise of titles like *Meat*, *Powertool* and *Like A Horse*. 'It's not natural', I reassured myself as I planned a trip to the nearest sex-shop in search of a penis enlarger. (Of course I know they don't actually *work*. Nor did Dumbo's magic feather, but that didn't do him any harm. It's all a question of confidence, dummy!)

Then I remembered the horror stories: the intrepid reporter who watched his knob racing excitedly down the glass tube only to come crashing through the end; the man who almost gave himself a coronary as a result of the rush of blood from the brain; the friend who reported total loss of erection powers after prolonged use of the vacuum pump he'd pinned such enormous hopes on. This was my greatest anxiety. When the day came, would I rise to the occasion? It's all very well saying size doesn't matter. We all know there are few things less attractive, or more ridiculous, than a limp dick.

If you're beginning to think this all sounds a trifle self-indulgent, well you're probably right, but my research tells me I'm not the only one who spends inordinate amounts of time worrying about dick-size. Take the defenders of law and order. British law is notoriously vague on matters of obscenity. Under the obscure terms of the Obscene Publications Act, the police are at liberty to confiscate 'indecent' materials likely to embarrass 'the ordinary citizen'. In the absence of more explicit guidance than this, Scotland Yard's Obscene Publications Branch have their own rule of thumb for identifying 'obscene' materials. Depictions of anal, oral, child, animal and group sex are among the main taboo subjects. So are erections.

A spokesman for the Obscene Publications Branch tells me, 'A photo in a magazine of a male with an erection will not necessarily be classified as obscene under the Obscene Publications Act. But as a general rule, any picture showing a fully erect penis will be seized and referred to magistrates.' With the police running around seizing all these erect penises, what the poor, overburdened magistrates are expected to do with them is anybody's guess. Send them down? Offer them a conditional discharge? I've often wondered what the men in wigs make of all these male appendages. We've all heard of judges nursing erections as they condemn the prostitute in the dock to three years' hard labour. What happens when it's a delinquent male member that's up for inspection? Do they run through a personal check list? Does penis envy play a part? Do they take pity on the smaller ones? Do they apply greater or lesser degrees of leniency, depending on the degree to which the offender defies gravity? You can see there are a lot of angles to consider.

A man I know at the BBC was making a film that involved a fair bit of male nudity. He had an idea that erections might play a significant role in the drama, and was a little confused by conflicting opinion about what constituted an offensive member. He'd heard the one about 'The Mull Of Kintyre'. (Nothing to do with Paul McCartney's inflated bank balance, merely a rumour that anything below the angle at which the peninsula protrudes from the mainland is permissible in the eyes of the law.) Envisaging total chaos, with maps of Great Britain littering the set, he contacted his own personal censor, the Broadcasting Standards Council, for guidance. 'An erection', came the reply, 'is defined as a vertically self-sustaining member.' Here was the creative challenge! Maybe the actor could just hold on to it? Better still, maybe he could make like a contortionist, angle his body so that his erection extended horizontally?

Censorship is a mind-bending business. According to all official sources, censors are there to protect us from materials which, were we exposed to them, would 'deprave' and 'corrupt' us. By my reckoning, that must make the esteemed members of the British Board of Film Classification (BBFC), who routinely subject themselves to such materials on our behalf, the most depraved and corrupt individuals that walk god's earth. At any rate, they're a funny bunch. Established in 1912 by the film industry, the Board's categories for film ratings have only ever been advisory. However, under the terms of the 1984 Video Recordings Act, its video ratings are legally binding. Under the present system, all video works must be submitted to the Board for censorship – even the ones that have been transmitted on television, or previously classified for cinematic release.

Now here is where it might be worth having a pen and paper handy. The only videos to escape the scrutiny of the Board are those that can claim educational merit, or are concerned with sport, religion or music. However, even videos which fall into these categories must be submitted if 'to any significant extent' they deal with 'human sexual activity'. Artistic merit doesn't come into it. Confused? Try looking at it this way: Madonna was awarded an 18 for her artistic endeavours in *Justify My Love*; *Cliff Richard Sings Stars on Sunday* would probably get away with an exemption certificate.

The release in 1991 of *The Lovers' Guide* seemed to mark a significant change of heart at the BBFC. Here was a video that featured explicit scenes of masturbation, 'creative' sexual positions, actual sexual intercourse (involving the elusive erect penis) – all things that would never be permitted in a feature film. Speaking at a conference on sex and censorship at the Institute for Contemporary Arts in April 1992, the Board's director, James Ferman, defended their decision to grant *The Lovers' Guide* an 18 certificate on the basis of its educational merit. It was, he said, 'justified as being for the public good' under the terms of the Obscene Publications Act. The subtext to this, of course, is that 'education', with its intimations of aspiration and hard graft, is far worthier and more defensible a pursuit than mere 'pleasure' – the indulgence of which, as we all know, is a sure route to the breakdown of Western civilization as we know it. To put it another way, it is perfectly acceptable for a penis to rise up in the name of self-improvement, but not for it to stand up and simply entertain.

What is plain for all to see is that the censors and law enforcers are running one hell of a protection racket. But who is being protected, and from what? The police claim to be in the business of protecting us, either from ourselves (try the old 'It's for your own protection ma'am' line) or, when that doesn't wash, from 'the worst elements in society' (in this case, the 'evil' pornographers). The BBFC claim, in their paternal wisdom, to have the interests of women and children at heart. But do either they or the law makers really think women would be mortally wounded if an erection popped up on telly, or between the pages of a magazine? Of course not. Is the sight of an aroused male member expected to transform a law-abiding female citizen into a marauding sex-beast? No, but we're getting warmer.

The way things currently stand, the symbolic phallus carries a lot of clout in our culture. But what would happen if erect penises became as over-exposed as, say, Samantha Fox's breasts? Picture the scene in the family home. Husband, wife and two-point-four kids sitting around the breakfast table and there, laid out next to the toast-rack, is the Page Three Fella. With a stiffy. Now it may well be that this isn't the sort of thing many women want to contemplate over breakfast, but spare a thought for what poor hubby must be going through. The shock of seeing his own sex displayed like that! The pain of knowing that some man, somewhere, has let the side down, has laid the naked truth on the line. Or at any rate the tablecloth.

The day before I let the side down, I carried out a quick survey of the men in the office. I should point out here and now that they're a pretty reconstructed bunch – sensitive to their girlfriends' 'needs' , each in touch with his own 'feminine side', that sort of thing. Traitors to a (new) man, most said they'd happily pose nude 'if the price was right', but could envisage 'all sorts of difficulties' when it came to getting an erection. Only one admitted to being 'shy about my dick'. About what exactly, I pushed. Its length? Its girth? The mystery attached to it? 'The mystery', he said quickly. But then he would say that, wouldn't he?

The morning of the photo-session I awoke, as usual, with a hard-on. Just hang on in there, I thought, as I raced off to the gym to ensure a bit of definition in some, if not all, departments. A couple of hours later, I'm standing in my underwear in a brightly-lit room somewhere in Pimlico. The make-up artist has expertly concealed the bags under my eyes, but no amount of cosmetics can hide the fact that there's nothing much happening down below. On the sets of porn films they have people called 'hardeners' ('*hard-on*-ers'?) whose job it is to keep spirits up. I find myself wondering how they're selected, what they talk about between takes, whether having one here would make any difference. 'How are you doin'?' asks Della, the embodiment of care and understanding. I've got my hand stuck down the front of my pants, desperately trying to solicit some response from my too, too temporal flesh. 'Not too good', I confess. Having taken the bull so firmly by the horn, I can feel myself slipping helplessly, hopelessly, into an inert state of bovine resignation.

I can't understand it. Normally, the only requisite to my having an erection is being in a horizontal position. We've tried everything. Lying on my back. Lying on my front. Resting against a chair. Leaning against the wall. We even toyed with the idea of a cock ring, but decided against it. It's not something I'm used to. With four people in the room, including two I'd never met before, I figured familiarity came before novelty. Subdued lighting was out of the question. We tried a bit of gentle coaxing, massage, self-genital-stimulation. Nothing.

Della suggests that everyone leave the room while I prepare myself for action. I try applying the first rule of algebra – the more you think about it, the harder it gets. Sex is between the ears, not the legs. Think, man, think! It works. I call out to Della ('Look, mom, no hands!'). She rushes back in. Everyone takes position. The lights go on, the lens is focused. The excitement is too much. We – or rather, I – lose it. Commiserations all round, but I'm not willing to throw in the towel now. In a last ditch attempt to dampen my inhibitions, I turn to the bottle. Quarter of an hour later, Della gets a few shots of my manhood looking less than impressive at half-mast. I blame it on the drink. It provoked the desire, it took away the performance. Given the right circumstances . . .

But then I would say that, wouldn't I?

Part two

Stars

Rescue Me: Sex, Subculture and the Material Girlie

I HAVE to start with a confession: I didn't think I'd last the whole two hours. That's how long reviewers were given to probe Madonna's *Sex*, published worldwide in October 1992. First you were asked to sign a contract, swearing you wouldn't breathe a word about the ambitious blonde's breathless affair with Steven Meisel's lens before the day the book was published. Then you were offered a pair of strong scissors (to cut your way through the celebrated, heavy-duty, heat-sealed packaging), a cup of strong tea (in case you couldn't hack it), and left to experience the pleasures of *Sex* at your own pace.

I have to admit I expected it all to be over in fifteen minutes. It's the same old story: male sexuality comes in short concentrated bursts, women have the capacity to go on and on. Madonna keeps on going for longer than most. In the first of her 'Letters to Johnny', which make up one strand of the accompanying text, she describes how she and her girlfriend 'Ingrid' have been finger-fucking each other for the past couple of hours, and how she's feeling all 'squishy' inside. A couple of pages on, she recollects her first gushing orgasm: 'that glorious day when finger found flesh and with legs spread open and back arched, honey poured from my 14-year-old gash and I wept'. You've got to hand it to her. When it comes to selling sex, nobody does it better. Or wetter.

22: *Stars*

It didn't take Madonna long to soothe away my initial anxieties. I was anticipating something along the lines of those awful *Vanity Fair* pictures, the ones that showed her prancing about in pigtails and a child's rubber ring. I was half expecting to see her reinforcing every dumb baby-doll image of available feminity. But those pictures were only a temporary distraction. In *Sex*, more than in anything she has done before or since, Madonna indulges her appetite for a bit of the Other: interracial sex, lesbian sex, sadomasochistic sex, anal sex, group sex, sex with switch-blades, sex with gay men, sex with old men, even the vague suggestion of sex with an alsatian.

Remember George Michael's desperate attempt at courting controversy? 'Sex is natural, sex is fun', he sang, as he wrestled under the sheets with his very own china girl. Well, there's no arguing with that. But then came the cop-out clause. Just when you thought he'd finally outgrown the silly notion that guilty body parts have got no rhythm, just when you thought he was about to live up to the promise of his old 'Bad Boy' image, he had to go and spoil it all by singing, 'sex is better when it's one on one'.

One of the best things about Madonna's *Sex* is that its star and author makes no attempt to justify the promiscuous pleasures of being such a bad girl. (In this sense, she was absolutely right to point out that *Sex* the book and *Erotica* the album actually had very little in common. For all its deep, throaty solicitations, *Erotica* says more about longing and regret than it does about pleasure. On the song 'Bad Girl' Madonna even confesses to feeling 'not happy' about acting the slut.) When George Michael sang 'I Want Your Sex', it was funk without spunk, a careless whisper he thought better of before he'd even reached the second chorus. When Madonna says she wants us to enjoy her *Sex*, she commits it to paper in block letters two inches high: 'I'll Teach You How To Fuck'. And unless you count her opening reminder that 'safe sex saves lives', there's nothing careless about it.

Of course carelessness has never been a part of Madonna's game-plan. You might well have laughed (I certainly did) at the absurd level of security surrounding the publication of what is, essentially, a book full of naughty – sometimes silly – photos. But in retrospect it seems only fitting that Madonna alone should have decided when, and under what conditions, her body was exposed for scrutiny by the world media. The marketing of *Sex* was the ultimate striptease, the publishing equivalent of a peep show, the next logical step in a career that has evolved around images of concealment and disclosure, from tantalizing glimpses of her midriff to the invitation to join her 'In Bed'.

The most revealing thing about the reception of *Sex* in Britain was the lengths most male journalists were prepared to go to, just to avoid the slightest acknowledgement of what was staring them in the face: that the girl they'd all been getting off on just a few years before had found herself a new playground, where boys like them would have a hard time fitting in. Instead we were informed, *ad nauseum*, of how *Sex* was proof of what they had suspected all along – that if Madonna means anything at all, she means business (given her peculiar habit of drawing attention to her own immodest ambitions, they might as well have pointed out that the empress wasn't wearing any clothes). So we saw the word 'hype' trailed across a hundred headlines. So we learned everything there is to know about a tear-resistant material called mylar. So we scanned pages of copy for the slightest mention of the material girl's moral objective in exposing herself to such extreme objectification (something about reaching out and touching up and thereby making the world a better place).

Personally, I am inclined to put this down to nothing more sinister than an infertile imagination. Academics like Cathy Schwichtenberg would doubtless interpret it as proof of a media conspiracy, an extension of the popular press strategy for diminishing Madonna's cultural and political significance by casting her as the ultimate 'low-Other'. The apparent tension between the 'practitioners of slanted journalism' (Madonna-haters) and the defenders of 'unbiased' critical engagement (Madonna-scholars) is just one of the binary oppositions present in *The Madonna Connection* – a collection of academic essays published in Britain a month after *Sex* and dedicated, so Schwichtenberg explains in her introduction, to demonstrating 'Madonna's usefulness as a paradigm to advance further developments in cultural theory' by exploring the star's relationship to various 'subcultural' groups (identified as blacks, lesbians, gay men, feminists).

What this really amounts to is an exercise in naked opportunism – which, given the nature of the subject, seems to me entirely excusable. Far harder to forgive is the tendency towards wild exaggeration (summed up in E. Ann Kaplan's invention of the 'MP' or 'Madonna Phenomenon'), and gross sentimentalizing of what is, after all, only pop music (see for example, Melanie Morton's 'Don't Go For Second Sex, Baby!', in which a fairly good pop tune is transformed, note-by-note, into a 'decimation' of 'patriarchal, racist and capitalist constructions').

While it is hardly a secret that Madonna forges many of her boldest mass-media representations from the effects of marginal cultures, it is an interesting sign of the times to see this construed as representing anything other than her own interests. When Elvis laid the populist base of rock 'n' roll by coming on like a negro, people accused him of capitalizing on the oppression of the black underclass. When Madonna gets down to the sounds and styles of black musical tradition, academics are inclined to applaud her 'acknowledgement and celebration of African musical roots'. So the sensation-seeking video for 'Like A Prayer' is vindicated on the grounds that it advocates 'the positive role of the black church in the lives of all it touches' (with extra brownie points awarded for its narrative incitement to viewers to 'do the right thing'). So the video for 'Vogue' is scrutinized for visual references to contemporary black films (in particular Isaac Julien's *Looking For Langston*), while little or no attention is paid to the fact that, for a song which borrows so heavily from black gay culture as a means to celebrating its singer's own narcissism, the lyrics are remarkably short of explicit references to black style-setters. Marilyn and Marlene are both mentioned (of course), but where are the legions of black divas who 'gave good face'? Where are Josephine Baker, Billie Holiday, Nina Simone?

In defence of Madonna's 'ambivalence' over what she describes as 'racial markers' in 'Vogue', Cindy Patton argues that the video's 'coherent allegiance to highly evocative race and gender codes suggests that the video's politic is less a pluralistic vision of essential humanity beneath race and gender than a postmodern resurfacing of signs in a way that produces race and gender as only skin deep'. Which, when you sit down and really think about it, is a bit like saying you should thank your lucky stars Madonna has at least given you a sign on which to pin your hopes of ever being fully represented.

Of course Madonna isn't nearly as interested in the politics of representation as she is the representation of her own pleasures. It isn't hard to see why queers just can't help falling deeper and deeper in love with Madonna – after all, who else can we rely on to slip some queer sex to 'the boys on MTV'? (Not George Michael, certainly.) But however much we might believe in the power of Madonna to rescue us from the margins, our faith is nothing compared to Madonna's faith in the power of queer sex to rescue her from the banality that dogs her every move. Madonna didn't get where she is today purely by accident. In her own words, she knows how to 'press people's buttons'. In the words of Julie Burchill, 'she looks like a whore and thinks like a pimp'. Sex is what Madonna deals in, and she isn't always bothered whether it is hers to sell, or somebody else's.

If coming on like a Boy-Toy is no longer guaranteed to shock anyone besides Mary Whitehouse, it's probably because heterosexuality, for all its little kinks, simply isn't that interesting – at least not to the vast majority of heterosexuals. Madonna knows this. She also knows that a little queerness can go an awfully long way. The extent of her borrowing from the queer image bank was never more clearly stated than it was in *Sex*, or in the subsequent *Girlie Show*. The question is, whose interests are really being served? In *Sex* she is pictured gasping in horror at the spectacle of two tattooed dykes getting it on. In the tour programme for the *Girlie Show* she invites the 'ladies and gentlemen' in the audience to 'step right up' and witness some 'freaks of nature'. In Madonna's book, lesbians and gay men are clearly fabulous, but that's 'fabulous' as in 'fantastical', not 'fabulous' as in 'FABULOUS!'

Ask me how Madonna figures in my view of the world, and I would say it goes something like this. Madonna is A Good Thing because she is sex-positive, because she takes an active role in the fight against AIDS, because she flirts with queer sexuality in a way few other contemporary pop performers would dare. Madonna is A Bad Thing because her *Sex* book is fully of petty prejudices about people who don't conform to her idea of physical beauty, because her only musical comment on AIDS is a soppy ballad that inspires nothing so much as passivity, because her flirtation with queerness always leaves her in the position to step back and deny any real involvement (like when she explained to a salivating Jonathon Ross that all that stuff about ass-fucking and muff-diving in *Sex* was just an 'irrelevant' 'joke').

The point I'm really trying to make is that Madonna is neither purely one thing nor purely another – neither a virgin nor a whore, neither a perfectly modern queer champion nor a totally old-fashioned culture vulture. The refusal to take stock of her contradictions is what made Ilene Rosenzweig's *I Hate Madonna Handbook* such an excruciating bore, but it is also what leaves so much Madonna scholarship sorely lacking in the scholarship department. Nobody with a real interest in popular culture would deny that Madonna's slippery exterior is worthy of concentrated penetration – it's the intellectual 'slippage' I just can't be doing with. In the course of arguing that Madonna's flirtation with 'Otherness' succeeds in shifting the politics and pleasures of minority con-stituences into the centre of the popular arena, the proponents of 'MP' ('Madonna Phenomenon') regularly fall into the trap laid by 'PM' ('Postmodernism'), wherein personal playfulness and the pur-suit of notority are misconstrued as political interventionism. For all its talk about sexual revelation and revolution, the most revealing sentence in *The Madonna Connection* is the one where Cathy Schwichtenberg offers thanks to Madonna for 'stirring up trouble and forcing us to think seriously about the politics of popular culture'. The plain fact of the matter is that for as long as Madonna continues to dodge the responsibilities of authenticity ('*Like* A Virgin', '*Like* A Prayer', or, more recently, '*Like* A Lesbian'), her genuflections to racial or sexual equality will only ever amount to a plastic pop revolution. Or something very like one.

Jason Talks Straight

Interview with Jason Donovan, July 1992

JASON Donovan is being pulled in two directions. 'At the age of twenty-three, a part of you wants to be respected by your peers. You want your friends to come up to you and say, "Shit! I heard your song on the radio last night. Sounds great! Gonna go out and buy it!" But the truth is, they're not gonna do that. You've got to realize who your audience is. People make the mistake of thinking they have to dump the young audience and earn respect from their peers. I don't believe in that. They are your peers in ten years' time. That's the important thing.'

It certainly sounds sincere – if not entirely logical ('They are your peers in ten years' time'? Who does he think he is? Dorian Gray?). Still, Jason Donovan ought to be pretty sure of his routine by now. He's peddled this line so many times, it won't be terribly long before he starts believing it himself. Moments later, he's giving the game away, blushing with pride as he informs me that friends have started asking for tickets to see *Joseph*. 'It's the first time in my life that's ever happened!' he gushes, grinning from ear to ear, revealing one of the least likely sets of pearly whites in pop history.

After a brief stint as a fair imitation of a Weetabix, the gravity-defying coiffure is back to a more natural shade of blond. He has a golden tan (of course) and looks fitter than you might expect, given the punishing nature of his daily schedule. He's running rather late today, after being caught up at the recording studio where they're rushing to get the whole of *Joseph* down on tape while the single 'Any Dream Will Do' is still riding high in the charts. He has spent the last hour being interviewed by a sheep called Nobby for a Saturday morning kids' show called *Ghost Train*, and has a man from the *Daily Express* to fit in before his 6.30 wig-fitting.

It's five o'clock in the afternoon, we're sitting in his dressing room at the London Palladium, and young Mr Donovan's make-up is showing signs of caking around the eyes. Not that it matters a hell of a lot. At close range, he is absurdly handsome. He is also disarmingly modest, charming, eager to please, etc. In short, Jason Donovan is too good to be true, which probably accounts for the fact that while one half of the world was wetting its pubescent knickers at the mere mention of his name, the other half was itching to see him fall flat on his financially lucrative face.

All the more to his credit, then, that our golden boy has made the transition from adored teen-idol to critical stage success while avoiding the kind of fleecing some would say is long overdue. A year before *Joseph* went into rehearsal, he confounded the critics' suggestions that he couldn't really sing by taking his brand of frothy pop on the road and getting by admirably without the aid of artificial sweeteners. A month before our meeting, accusations of lip-synching surrounded his big opening in the West End. But dammit, he's done it again, turning the limits of his talent to his advantage by putting in a splendidly self-effacing performance as Joseph in Stephen Pimlott's knowing production. It might not sound like an earth-shattering achievement, but bear in mind that neither of the two Donny's (Osmond or Wahlberg) could have gotten away with it.

'The reviews really surprised me, actually', says Jason, the vaguest hint of a frown hovering across his brow, the absolute picture of earnestness. 'I expected them to be bad. I sort of expected people to really have a go. It was their great opportunity to see me make a fool of myself, wearing a wig and everything. I guess I thought, because it isn't *Phantom of the Opera*, because it isn't *Equus* or a play like that, I thought it would just be too obvious for the critics to like it. It's a really thin story, about a guy who works hard and wins through. *Joseph* is the story of a dreamer, a bit of an innocent who is insecure, but who ultimately believes in what he does and becomes successful as a result.'

Which makes it a timely revival for the idealistic 1990s, and the perfect vehicle for a popster who, in spite of the celebrated loincloth and the undesirable attentions of the tabloids, would prefer to have us go on believing that he really is the wide-eyed boy next door. 'It was never an image I painted for myself,' he insists. 'It's an image that the press painted on me. But I guess it's not a bad image to have. I'm certainly more proud of it than I would be of being a smacked-out rock freak. I mean, why do so many pop stars put on leather jackets and put ear-rings in their ears, and then go home and put on a pair of track pants and sit around doing the normal things people do? Why be different as soon as you walk through the door? I mean, I just believe in being myself – y'know? I'm just growing up naturally.'

Well, perhaps not entirely. Growing up naturally under the glare of the media is no mean feat, as the former Bondi Beach boy knows only too well. 'It's tough', he acknowledges in a little voice. 'Anyone in my position who ever says to you that they love it and wouldn't want to do anything else is telling a lie. There are times when I think I'd love to just work in a shop, and clock in and clock out. But . . .' He pauses. Obviously it's going to be a big but. 'But I know that as soon as I got to do it, I'd probably hate it.'

Ask him about the drugs stories and the speculation about his sexuality and he immediately puts his guard up, leans back, arms crossed. There is a moment's silence while he ponders what to say, and I ponder my chances of not being ejected from the room. When he does speak, he forms his words slowly and deliberately. He's been this way before. 'The success of this show and the success of the single just goes to show how thin those rumours were. If people were to have believed what they read, I'm pretty sure they wouldn't have taken to what I've done as well as they have.'

He pauses again. Perhaps he's realized that this line of argument is getting neither of us anywhere. He tries another tack. 'Look, it's unfair for people to say things like being gay, or the drugs thing, y'know? I don't take drugs, and I'm not gay. Some of my best friends are gay, I'm not denying that. But it's not the way I choose to live my life. To convince people of that just isn't worth the bother. Let them think it if that's what they want to think.'

It's a far cry from statements he's given previously. What, no mention of his alleged affair with Kylie, no surfing tales? 'I just said, "this is the situation" ', he insists. 'Believe it, or don't believe it. That's me, y'know? That's me about my career. That's me about my image. If you like it, buy it. If you don't, don't.'

Some people aren't buying it. A few weeks before our meeting, a spate of posters appeared across London, signalling the arrival of an outing campaign similar to those being waged in the United States. Donovan is depicted with the slogan 'Queer As Fuck' emblazoned across his chest. Was he aware that he had become the target of radical queer activism?

He mumbles a vague 'no', accompanied by much rearranging of hair. 'In, er, London? Really? What's it all about?' I dutifully explain the principles of outing, though I have a distinct recollection of Donovan discussing said campaign with Michelle Collins on *The Word*. Perhaps it slipped his mind. 'So it's basically gay rights', he interrupts. 'It's funny. The thing is, without getting into this, because I really don't want to, the thing is, there is nothing wrong with homosexuality, absolutely nothing wrong with it at all. I don't deny people the privilege or the right to do whatever. It's a free world. It just frustrates me that people in that position would want to think of you as one of them. That's what frustrates me, when you know damn well, and they know damn well, that you're not gay. That's where it gets my back up a bit.' He halts and shrugs his shoulders. 'C'est la vie.'

We spend the remaining five minutes negotiating our way towards a polite departure point, briefly discussing his immediate plans (a holiday) and future direction. 'The great thing about this business', he says, 'is that creatively there are no limits. Same with art, same with music, same with all those bits and pieces. There are no boundaries, really, no rules. I think I've shown that I'm as capable of doing *Joseph* as someone who may have spent five or six years treading the boards.'

I take this as my cue to pack up and leave. Jason Donovan barely has time to compose himself before the man from the *Daily Express* appears at the door. Halfway back to the office, I suddenly remember that I meant to ask him about the photographs of Chesney Hawkes plastered around his bathroom mirror. Still, it's nice to see our Jase taking the competition so seriously.

My Own Private Keanu

JUST what is it that makes today's homo-icons so different, so appealing? Back in the mid-1980s, a young brat-packer called Rob Lowe introduced me to an acquaintance of his – a spotty, greasy-haired adolescent by the name of Keanu Reeves.

Though he'd never expressed the slightest interest in my existence, my affair with Rob Lowe had been going strong for three years. It began when I was first offered a glimpse of his smooth, toned body muscling in beside Matt Dillon, the official star of Francis Ford Coppola's 1983 teen-angst flick *The Outsiders*. By 1986, Rob was demanding starring roles of his own. *Youngblood* was a typical Rob Lowe vehicle. The pop-mythic account of a pretty boy's battle to assert his masculinity by becoming the star player in the local ice hockey team, it gave Rob plenty of scope for doing the things he did best: look pretty, work up a sweat and wander around locker rooms in various stages of undress. Stuck in a supporting role as a second-reserve member of the team, Keanu got twelfth billing, half a dozen lines, and less screen time than Rob's jockstrap.

Several naked butt-shots later, Rob's film career is at an all-time low. Keanu, on the other hand, has risen to the top of the Hollywood hip list. What's more, he appears to have made a few influential friends the likes of which Rob could only dream of making an impression on. I'm thinking here of the scores of seriously minded critics prepared to pay Keanu Reeves the same kind of attention they normally reserve for more overtly 'intellectually challenging' talents such as Madonna.

Barely thirty, Keanu Reeves is not only the most talked about actor of his age (*Sky* magazine seems to find something to say about him practically every month); he is also a fully fledged 'phenomenon', an 'icon' whose 'cultural significance' is weighed up everywhere, from the pages of *The Modern Review* to the lecture halls of the Art Centre College of Design, Pasadena, where students are invited to 'use Reeves' films as a departure point for discussing culture and philosophy'. (Naturally, the college authorities are keen to stress the rigorous academic discipline of the course on offer, pointing out that students would be treated to a screening of, say, *Bill & Ted's Excellent Adventure* only as a means to helping them engage with the arguments outlined in Michel Foucault's essay on Nietzsche.)

Asked to comment on his new-found role as a learning aid, Keanu was characteristically laid back. 'I guess I'm not really involving my imagination to that', he told a reporter recently. 'I'm just kind of acknowledging it as an existence.' If only his fans in media-land could display a similar degree of reserve when it came to filing their copy. Rarely do you read anything concerning Keanu that doesn't end in an exclamation mark. He's hot! He broods! He sneers! His name means 'cool breeze over a mountain'! He has wit, intellect and devastating good looks! He uses words like 'boda-cious'! He rides a 1972 Combat Norton motorbike! He sometimes takes his clothes off!

And he's very, very popular with gay men. When Greg Gorman persuaded him to pose naked for a photo session, the evidence found its way on to the walls of homosexual abodes the world over. Armistead Maupin made reference to his boyish good looks in *Maybe the Moon*. Dennis Cooper made a fetish of his blank allure in *Frisk* (though it seems unlikely that even a dreamboat as apparently heavily sedated as Keanu would take kindly to being the object of a necrophiliac's fantasies). John Patrick, editor of *The Year in Sex*, an annual gay glossary of hunks and heart-throbs, made a meal of 'his delicious lips, armpits, eyes and waist'. Even bitchy old Sandra Bernhard (whose talent for passing off spiteful remarks as cutting-edge humour makes her more of a gay man than a lesbian) was moved to speak kindly on the subject of his extraordinary (some would say, inexplicable) popularity. 'He has the look of jailbait, and that's damn sexy', Sandra said not so long ago. 'He's a kooky kid, admittedly short on cultural references, but I dig him that way.'

It would be nice to present a case for Keanu's queer appeal as evidence of gay men's heightened sensitivity and acute cultural awareness. So I won't. Besides, there really isn't much to go on. Whatever Keanu's natural endowments, rumours of his skills as an actor are greatly exaggerated. According to the *Who's Who in Hollywood*, he is 'a performer of some range and versatility'. Appraising his career in a 'Fan Letter' for *The Modern Review* last year, Polly Frost displayed all the blind passion of the true fanatic, arguing that 'it isn't easy to strip away your defenses as a performer', and used words like 'subtle', 'original' and 'honest' to describe Keanu's performances in a few of her favourite films.

'Crap' would have been closer to the truth. Pitifully limited in his range of expressions, Keanu is only ever remotely persuasive playing variations on his own, admittedly attractive, boy-man persona. His most successful roles were as the troubled teen in *River's Edge* (1987), the teen whose best friend tops himself in *Permanent Record* (1988), the goofy teen in *Bill & Ted's Excellent Adventure* (1989) and in the dodgy follow-up *Bill & Ted's Bogus Journey* (1991).

The trouble with teen roles is that they tend to dry up the day your skin starts crying out for liposomes. Judging from the parts he's been chasing lately, Keanu appears to have taken note. But try as he might, he isn't terribly convincing when he's required to act like a man. This is particularly true when the man in question hails from any part of the world other than California. Accents have never been Keanu's strong point, which goes some way to explaining why he was so dreadful as Jonathan Harker in Coppola's *Dracula*. English accents are notoriously difficult for Americans to fake in any case. Add to that the demands of pretending not to notice when his hair kept changing colour and you can probably see why it all proved too much for the poor boy.

Sadly, he can't offer the same excuse for his performance in Kenneth Branagh's colour-balanced but boring *Much Ado About Nothing* (1993). Part of the problem here seems to have been that his role as Don John the Bastard didn't actually require him to act, merely to strut about looking moody and magnificent. It is through Keanu's often bungled attempts at fleshing out a character that he usually ends up revealing the most attractive parts of himself (what Polly Frost refers to as 'his natural physical gifts'). Worse still, the cosmetic demands of the role ruled out any possibility of falling back on his boyish charms. The come-to-bed eyes were set in a hard stare; the goofy grin was hidden beneath an even harder beard. Branagh must have recognized the problem. As a cheap concession to Keanu's worshippers, the director had him strip off for a massage. But even with all that baby oil glistening on his chest he looked too suspiciously adult, too grown up to be a proper boy-toy.

Of course, the first step to understanding Keanu Reeves's place in gay men's hearts (and loins) is to accept that acting has very little to do with it. 'Young, dumb and full of come' is how his embodiment of an FBI agent was described by a fellow cop character in *Point Break* (1991), Kathryn Bigelow's heavily iconic, cheerfully ironic take on the buddy action movie, centred on a gang of bank-robbing surfers. Keanu played the improbably named Johnny Utah, an undercover cop assigned to penetrate the surfers' ring – though for much of the film he looks as though he'd much rather be penetrated by the gang leader, played by Patrick Swayze. Relying on Keanu's curiously passive, vaguely androgynous quality to subvert the macho excesses of the storyline, Bigelow was rewarded with the best adult performance Keanu has given – and the most easily appropriated in gay terms. A sperm-fest of surf, sweat and male bonding rituals, *Point Break* was to homoerotica what Bigelow's earlier *Blue Steel* was to dykey androgyny. Despite the fact that homosexual acts never fully enter the picture, it remains the queerest thing that Keanu has committed himself to.

Queerer, certainly, than his retentive performance as Scott, the 'Prince Hal' of Portland, in Gus Van Sant's *My Own Private Idaho* (1991). Now available to rent (and buy), *Idaho* has Keanu hawking his ass while resisting the affections of fellow hustler Mike (played with scene-stealing sensitivity by the late lamented River Phoenix). 'I only have sex with guys for money', Scott mumbles when Mike declares his undying love. 'Two guys can't love each other'. Gay men being the contradictory creatures they are, this was the performance which resulted in legions of queens fantasizing about their own private Keanu.

If *Idaho* saw Keanu taking his desirability very much for granted, his latest film *Speed* (1994) looks set to cement his reputation as a major box office draw. A 1970s disaster movie cunningly disguised as a 1990s action thriller, *Speed* has Keanu butching it up as Jack Traven, a fearless LAPD cop trapped on a runaway city bus set to explode the moment the speedometer falls under 50 mph. Never mind that his performance is exceptionally bad – even for a genre in which bad acting is the rule that gives exceptional talents the opportunity to prove themselves. Never mind that the bus is the real star of the film. *Speed*'s success in America has already given rise to the tabloid myth that Keanu Reeves is the greatest action hero since, well, the last one.

And of course the greatest irony of all is that this is probably the film that will win him back all those gay fans put off by his ridiculous beard in *Much Ado About Nothing* and ridiculous hairdo in *Little Buddha* (1994). With his gym-toned body and number two crop, Keanu's appearance in *Speed* is the best facsimile yet of all that gay men desire: an action man with gripping hands and eager, come-fuck-me eyes. Sadly, we don't actually get to see much of the body. He never gets around to taking his shirt off. And this being a 'straightforward' sort of action movie, the only desires represented on screen are resolutely heterosexual. But when did that ever make a blind bit of difference?

What, exactly, is the queer appeal of Keanu Reeves? I think that great queer theorist Kenneth Branagh probably summed it up best when he remarked that 'Keanu has an aloof quality, a far-away quality. You can't quite get close to him, he is somehow unattainable. That makes him very, very attractive. He seems to display all the qualities one would want: a very sexy, erotic, physical being. And yet he's got something at the back of his eyes that says, "No, I won't be committing here." He'll always be on the bus, heading off.'

Boys Keep Swinging

GEORGE Michael says he doesn't really mind if people think he does it, but declines to confirm or deny the rumours. The late Kurt Cobain used to run around spraying walls with slogans claiming that he did it all the time – but that was just to annoy the neighbours. David Bowie either used to do it back in the days when anybody who was anybody did it (purely for artistic reasons, you understand), or only *pretended* that he did, depending on which 'exclusive' interview you read around the time of 'Black Tie, White Noise'. And Brett Anderson of Suede is very keen to tell us that he hasn't actually done it, but possibly would given half a chance, and in any case it's cool to be flexible these days, innit?

The 'it' in question is gay sex. Buggery is back on the pop agenda. Not that it was ever really off it. In the mad, bad and dangerous world of pop, a little queerness has always gone a long way – but don't make too strong a case of it or you'll never be Big In America (witness Bowie's bank balance before he came over all sincere and serious, and started moonlighting as A Lad In A Suit).

Confession time. I'm one of those really sad individuals who used to believe in David Bowie (yeah, I know, but I was *soooo young*, okay?). I'm talking about the days when the thin white one used to get down on his knees to bite at the late lamented Mick Ronson's guitar strings, not to recite the Lord's Prayer. I'm talking about the days when 'I'm Only Dancing' was part of a pretty queer song title, not an excuse for cleaning up and selling out. I'm talking about the days when boys were really into swinging and we all thought a pop star's 'bisexual' confessions actually amounted to something.

Were I a few years younger and far less jaded, I'd probably find myself believing in Brett Anderson. Sorry, but I'm not, and I don't. It isn't that I don't have time for Suede's music (*Dog Man Star* was very possibly the best album of 1994). It isn't that I don't experience a little nostalgic thrill at every Bowiesque note (though it has to be said that Brett's brittle impersonation of Bowie isn't nearly as interesting as Bowie's brittle impersonation of Anthony Newley). It's just that, all things considered, Brett's ambiguous posturing means a damn sight less to me than Senseless Things putting out a record called *Homophobic Asshole*, or Nirvana putting a note on the sleeve of their *Insecticide* album which reads 'if any of you in any way hate homosexuals, people of different color, or women, please do this one favour for us – leave us the fuck alone!' I'm talking about that boring old word 'commitment', and I'm not seeing much evidence of it in the current fashion for limp hips and big girls' blouses.

Of course lack of commitment is something the new, improved, socially ware, 'real' David Bowie is very sensitive about. 'With gays it is very much us and them', he complained to *Arena* in May 1993. 'In the States, towards the end of the 70s, I think the gay body was pretty hostile toward me because I didn't seem to be supporting the gay movement in any kind of way. And I was sad about that.' Not nearly as sad as we were, Dave me old mucker. I mean, was it really too much to ask a man who had fashioned an entire career on the exploitation of queer subcultures to pay just a little lip service to the needs of those people he capitalized on? Saying a little prayer at the Freddie Mercury memorial concert hardly makes up for a lifetime's ducking and diving.

Reviewing Bowie's *Scary Monsters* album in the November 1980 issue of *The Face*, Jon Savage argued that Bowie's contribution to gay liberation was to open a Pandora's box of polymorphous possibilities: 'By making homosex *attractive* (rather than a snigger), he liberated and brought into the mainstream a whole range of fantasies which had hitherto been repressed. Naturally, they came out with great force.' Perhaps, but Bowie's posturing (and the fact that Ziggy Stardust never, in a sense, apologized) have to be weighed against Bowie's pronouncements (and the fact that the man himself was, in a sense, only too ready to). Nowadays, Bowie says he has 'a problem relating to my life and my sexuality in the early 1970s'. The 'problem' he speaks of is nothing new. As far back as 1972, at the height of his 'bisexual' phase, he was quoted as saying that he didn't know whether he was 'against or for Gay Lib'. Cheers, mate.

What line Brett will take when push comes to shove remains to be seen, but judging by his performance to date I'm not going to hold my breath. 'I see myself as a bisexual who has never had a homosexual experience', is his famous position on sexuality, and it's not a very comfortable one – for us, at least. Asked during an interview with *Gay Times* whether he was simply hijacking queer imagery, blousey Brett got a bit shirty: 'if you're asking me am I insincere to pose as a sodomite because I haven't had a cock up my arse, then no, I'm not.' Sorry Brett darling, but yes, you most certainly are. Some people might find your argument that 'the sexuality you express is not limited to things you've already experienced' just queer and dandy. Personally, I find it about as persuasive as hearing a New Man bleating on about how he 'empathizes' with his girlfriend's period pains. The bottom line is, pop would still sooner eat itself than admit to eating arse. When the boys who make a killing out of pop's fey days are prepared to flex some political muscle or take the risk that comes with living out a gay identity, then I'll see some cause for celebration. In the meantime, please – 'stop taking me over'.

I'll Grumble for Ya

Interview with Boy George, November 1993

BOY George is difficult. And he knows it. He said as much in the press release accompanying his greatest hits album, *At Worst . . . The Best of Boy George and Culture Club*: 'I'm older, wiser and still as difficult.'

And boy, don't I know it too. It's ten past five in the afternoon, I've been waiting patiently since half past three, and the first thing he says to me when I walk into the interview room at Virgin Records is: 'I hope you're better than the last one. He bored me senseless.' Aware of George's turbulent history with the press, and eager to start off on a good footing, I ask him what bores him (just so as I can try and avoid making the same mistakes). 'Talking about myself', he snaps back. My first impulse is to point out that this really leaves me very little scope. Instead, I try a little humour, suggest that we can always talk about me if he'd prefer, only it probably wouldn't make a very good interview. He doesn't laugh.

So for the first fifteen minutes of our alloted hour, we talk about everybody else. Madonna, for example. In George's opinion, 'she's a bit monotonous. She's not a great singer. I think Madonna the idea is more interesting than Madonna the musician. People are fascinated by her, and I can see why. But as a person I think she's pretty obnoxious.'

Matt Dillon's name crops up. I recollect reading somewhere that George met Matt at a party, and that the conversation turned to reincarnation. Matt asked George what he'd most like to come back as; George suggested a pair of Matt's knickers. 'Actually, that isn't what happened', George corrects me. 'I made that comment to a magazine. I actually met Matt Dillon at my twenty-fifth birthday party in New York. I asked him to come and sit next to me on the bed, and he didn't want to. I found him very unfriendly actually. I felt like, if you can't handle your own beauty, then cut your head off, honey.'

Next up for the chop is Andy Bell. George went to see Erasure perform at the then Hammersmith Odeon in 1992. He didn't like the show much: 'I was watching him, and I was thinking, they don't mind you being a queer so long as you're not being political. You can hoppity skip around the stage in your high heels and your little sequinned swimming costume, but so long as you're not actually challenging them, that's fine.'

I must have balked at this point, hearing Boy George of all people expressing such sentiments. He clocks my reaction, stares into the space in front of him. Embarrassed, I let my eyes wander around the room, take in the Culture Club posters and the Boy George dolls lined up neatly on the shelves. 'I suppose watching Andy Bell skipping around the stage like that reminded me of myself in Culture Club', George says. 'I got angry with him because he reminded me of myself.' And finally it dawns on me that for the past fifteen minutes, we've haven't really been talking about anybody else at all. We've been talking about Boy George all along.

To say that Boy George has trouble seeing beyond the end of his own nose is an understatement. Like most pop stars, George tends to think that the world revolves around him. Unlike most pop stars, he is at least willing to admit it. 'I'm a very selfish person on some levels', he confesses to me later, when I've got over my initial misgivings about this interview and he's got over his initial boredom. 'That's not all I am, but I can be very selfish.'

He is also prepared to admit that, despite his boasts about never having been 'hemmed in by any idea of how people should see me', his record on speaking out about gay identity isn't exactly inspiring. At first, he tries to fob me off with a few lines from a Depeche Mode song, the one that says 'words are very unnecessary, they can only do harm'. 'Anyone who saw me in my frocks on *Top of the Pops* and thought I was heterosexual obviously needed glasses!', he chortles. 'Everything about me was so obviously gay, in a way I didn't need to say it.'

Now it's my turn not to laugh. Because for all his flippancy, George knows as well as I do that, in the vernacular of pop, a little queerness can go a long way: it's the naming of it that can make or break a career. To put it another way, George clowning around in silly costumes was one thing, George drawing attention to the underlying seriousness of it all was quite a different ball-game. And one he wasn't prepared to risk losing. Hence his evasions, his quips about preferring a nice cup of tea to a good shag. You could say he was a man who knew how to sell a contradiction. He was, to all intents and purposes, a queen without a sexuality. Or, as he himself puts it, 'I was harmless. I was a safe commodity.'

Youth had a lot to do with it, of course. George was barely twenty-one when Culture Club made their first *Top of the Pops* appearance. And as he rightly says, 'when you're young, not only are you coming to terms with yourself and how you feel about your sexuality, you're also coming to terms with the way society treats you.' George believes that the decision to come out or not is one the individual must make for him or herself. And he argues very strongly that none of us has the right to sit in judgement: 'I agree that we need gay role models. But you also have to accept that it's a very difficult thing to do. Although I didn't openly say I was gay at the time, I think I changed a lot of people's lives. The funny thing about my success was that suddenly there were lots of little Georges every-where. So in a way I did my bit. Nowadays, when I go out to the clubs, I see a lot of my old fans, the ones who used to hang around the house and the recording studio. They're all out of the closet now, and they're almost embarrassed when they see me. But I know them. They can hide all they want under their checked shirts and their jeans. They can ignore me all they like. I know them.'

Some people George does his own level best to ignore. Like the woman who trailed him around the West End a few weeks ago. When she finally caught up with him, announcing that she knew who he was, George told her to piss off. 'There are days when I don't want that kind of hassle', he says simply. 'If I'm in Sainsbury's carrying six bags of shopping and somebody asks for my autograph, I think it's okay for me to just say "no". It's not the end of the world. If people ask me, "Are you Boy George?", I say, "Sometimes". By the time they've worked that one out, I'm gone.'

Still he wants to make it absolutely clear that, at heart, he's a people person. 'I love people', he says, with such an emphasis and such a passion that I half-expect him to break into a chorus of Barbara Streisand's 'People' at any moment. 'That's what the world is, y'know – people. They're a constant source of fascination for me. The things they come out with, the things they do. I never wanted to be one of those pop stars who drives over the fans in their limo. I'd hate to lose that contact with people.'

This push-and-pull seems typical of him. As much as he claims he never wanted to build a career on detachment, as much as he professes to enjoy being 'a normal shitting, pissing, bleeding human being like everyone else', there is a part of Boy George that loves and needs to be seen to be different, that couldn't bear the banality of simply being part of a social grouping. Hence the ambivalent streak that tempers his much-publicized religious passions. He says he hates the word 'religion' in any case, 'because it summons up images of dogma and all those things I really don't like. My spiritual beliefs are really haphazard. I'm hovering around the spiritual globe. I think Jesus Christ was a really cool guy with a really cool message. I'm interested in Buddhism and Krishna-consciousness. But it's difficult for me, because if you show an interest they want you to say "I'm a Hare Krishna" or "I'm a Buddhist". I feel very uncomfortable with those titles. I think you can be attracted to something without wanting to throw yourself into it one hundred per cent.'

He feels much the same way about being gay. He's written a few overtly gay political lyrics over the years (the rather humdrum 'No Clause 28', the magnificent 'Generations Of Love'), and believes that 'there are times in our lives when we have to fight for what we believe in'. Still, he says, 'you have to be careful not to get into a situation where nothing else matters. People get so wrapped up in issues, they can forget to be human. A lot of gay people walk around with a chip on their shoulder. What you have to do is believe in yourself, because when you believe in yourself, other people will believe in you. It sounds corny, but it's true. I suppose what I'm saying is, you can be too political. You can go to extremes. You can become obsessive.'

George sees a lot of obsessive behaviour in the gay world. Gay activists are 'obsessive', gay men who have casual sex are 'obsessive'. 'An awful lot of gay men are sexually obsessed,' he declares at one point. 'They use sex to assess themselves. People who go to Hampstead Heath, who go to toilets – they're terrified of intimacy, they're terrified of relationships. Part of us really believes that we are perverts, because that's the message that we've been given since we were born. Think about that. Think about it.' (I've thought about it, and I think it's a gross over-generalization.)

Later, when we are on the subject of hedonism and its effects on the gay club scene, he tells me he thinks escapism has a lot to do with it: 'It's not just AIDS. A lot of gay people come from dysfunctional families. There's violence, non-communication, loneliness. There are hundreds of things we're trying to escape from. That's what drugs are about. That's what sex can be about, too. Sex can be as much of a drug as cocaine, heroin or ecstasy. Cigarettes, alcohol, food, work, desire, lust – there's an endless supply of things out there to keep us from our problems. Maybe one will kill you quicker than the others, but apart from that there's really no difference.'

Sensing no small amount of personal projection in what he's saying, I ask George whether he considers himself to be an obsessive person. There is a pause before he answers: 'Yes. Definitely. I think I'm one of those people who has learned to judge myself by how people respond to me sexually.'

Sex. Drugs. Rock and roll. Boy George has had his fair share. He describes coming off heroin as the biggest turning point in his life. 'I wasn't a well woman for a long time after that', he says, shuddering at the thought. 'I'd fucked up and I felt really bad about it. When "Everything I Own" went to number one [in March 1987] it was like people were putting their arms around me. They were saying they still cared about me. They forgot about me very quickly afterwards, but at the time I saw the success of that single as a strong sympathy vote.'

Nowadays fame is the only regular fix he needs. He wouldn't admit to it, of course. He tries to persuade me that, while he enjoys the trappings of being famous, he doesn't take the lure of the limelight too seriously. But there's more than a trace of bitterness in his voice when he describes all the humble pie he's been forced to eat over the past five years, the tiny clubs he's played, the audiences who really didn't give a toss whether he came on or not. There have been occasions when he considered cancelling. 'But I always went on. I always go on. I've felt a real sense of ridicule at times, but all through that I believed that somehow I'd make it back. I'm not talking about being as successful as I was. I'm just talking about getting my life to work again. Because for a long time I didn't think it ever would'.

He recalls a particularly inauspicious gig in Newcastle, where fifty people showed up. The next night he was in Bournemouth. A local newspaper ran the headline 'Do You Really Want To Hurt Me? Boy George Plays To Fifty People.' 'That must have really injured your pride', I say in my best sympathetic voice. He laughs: 'Why should it? It's not my problem if people in Newcastle haven't got any taste.' The message is clear: Boy George is big – it's the audiences that got small.

He reckons he's got a far better perspective on things these days, largely due to the 'major amounts' of therapy he's put himself through over the past year. 'I feel like my eyes have been scrubbed', he says, staring out at me through lashings of mascara. 'I've always had a pretty big picture of the world, and of my experience, but since I've been in therapy it's become even bigger. If I had my way, I'd make therapy compulsory. Get it before you need it! It's an amazing experience ... ' He pauses, racks his brain for an example of the wisdom he has picked up. ' "The greatest truths are the simplest"', he announces solemnly. 'That's why they often go right over our heads. They seem so obvious. But if you actually sit down and think about them, they're terribly profound. They're earth-shattering. It's like this guy on my last therapy course told me: "It's really important to do ordinary things in an extraordinary way." It really struck me that you can live your life – whether you're a shoe-salesman, or you work in a canteen, or you're a pop star – you can live your life to the full and enjoy it, rather than moaning about what you haven't got. Because if you're not bankrupt in one department, then the chances are you're bankrupt in another.'

Financially speaking, George is a long way off bankruptcy, but isn't keen to talk figures: 'All I'll say is, I'm okay. You wouldn't believe how much money I wasted in the early days. When I went to see my accountant after the shit hit the fan, and he told me how much money I'd spent, I just laughed. But I did keep some. I wasn't that stupid.' Mentally speaking, he says he couldn't afford not to work again: 'I'd go mad.'

Since the success of the film *The Crying Game* (1992) put him back in the charts, George's output has been little short of prolific (though admittedly, this takes account of remixes of previously recorded tracks). He is more upfront now than he ever was in his heyday, choosing to write songs which reflect his experience rather than purely commercial considerations. He recently penned a song about his friend Stevie, who died of AIDS in 1991. 'It's something I've really had to face up to in the last few years', he says. 'In "Generations Of Love", I mentioned AIDS because it was really important for me to be able to say that word in a song. Since then I've been struggling to find a way of conveying how I feel about it. It was such a powerful experience for me, being around Stevie. His sense of humour was really unsettling. I think laughter can be a defence against a lot of things, including fear.'

He is also in the process of writing an autobiography, *Take It Like a Man*. He hesitates before divulging any details ('You'll just have to buy the book'), but can't resist the opportunity to dish the dirt on Jon Moss: 'Did you know he's got a girlfriend now? He's a funny bloke. He was great in bed, though. I knew nothing until I met him. He was fabulous. When I first met Jon it was brilliant for six months. I thought I'd met my prince. Then just as everything was coming together, just as we were getting a deal, he went off with this girl. And it was the way he did it. Right in front of my face, like I didn't matter, like I was a piece of shit. I was never able to trust him after that. So you can imagine what it was like. There was a lot of kicking and fighting behind the scenes. I was definitely obsessed with Jon. I knew that one day I'd get my revenge one way or other. And it's called "My Book"!'

He laughs at this, and for a few moments drifts off into his memories of the early 1980s and life as the frontman with a near-perfect pop group called Culture Club. 'You don't know the half of it', he says quietly, more to himself than to me. 'Did you know I used to go out with Kirk Brandon? The guy from Theatre Of Hate? He got married recently. I was really upset. I've written a song about it. That's how I write. I just walk along the road and bitterly think about the past.'

And then he laughs again. Very convincingly.

Butt Head

VIDEO killed the radio star, but it gave the action hero a new lease on life. Take Jean-Claude Van Damme. Before he muscled his way into the Hollywood mainstream with films like *Universal Soldier*, *Nowhere to Run* and *Hard Target*, Van Damme kicked around in a parallel universe, a twilight world known as STV (Straight To Video).

A word to the wise asses. STV might not be every action fan's idea of a postmodern paradise. There isn't much irony in a world where violent actions speak louder than words. There aren't many cute, clever, intertextual references in a world where budgets are low and directors with degrees in semiotics are pretty thin on the ground. Let's face it: this isn't the ideal setting for your thesis on *Textual Complexity and the Shifting Terms of Male Identification in Late-Twentieth-Century Cinema*. In STV, men are men, women are women, and performativity doesn't count for a hell of a lot. In STV, a man is judged to have given a meaningful performance if he can kick his way out of a paper bag.

With a dozen film credits to his name, 'the Muscles From Brussels' has shown he can do rather better than that. A world-class kickboxer long before he made the move into movies, Van Damme's durability as an action hero rides on the fact that he can kick himself out of practically any given situation. Critics who complain that his films all share the same basic storyline are missing the point of the exercise. What Van Damme movies lack in narrative originality they more than make up for in physical application. Iron bars, samurai swords, even sawn-off shotguns are no match for his flying feet. In *Cyborg*, he even kickboxed his way off a crucifix. And people accuse the man of lacking versatility?

Inevitably, such demonstrations of excessive physicality have landed Van Damme with a gay following. But his bodily functions (and the fact that he once played a gay kickboxing biker in the otherwise forgettable *Monaco Forever*) are only part of his queer appeal. It is Jean-Claude's willingness to share the story of his re-creation that strikes a chord with queens (such as I) who grew up suspecting that the Cinderella Complex wasn't just about girls with dirty faces and evil stepmothers. Of all the muscle-men who've staked a claim on celluloid, Van Damme is not only the prettiest by far, he is also the one most likely to divulge his deepest, darkest secrets. 'I was ugly when I was young', he confessed to an interviewer in 1991. 'Blond hair, big glasses – like a nerd. My father pushed me to do karate. Then I started to train very hard with weights. I was crazy about those 'Silver Surfer' and 'Spiderman' cartoons. I was dreaming of those guys with muscles.'

It's hardly surprising that a man prepared to let slip such an admission should also be willing to acknowledge his gay audience. 'Those people obviously have lots of taste', was his response when asked how he felt about being a gay icon. What's more, his films often acknowledge the fine line between kicking ass and licking ass. In *Lionheart*, an adversary tells him, 'You're kind of pretty. I don't know if I want to fuck you or fight you.' Jean-Claude wrote that line into the script himself. 'It's funny', he pointed out at the time. 'It builds a little tension before the fight.'

'The Fight' is the event around which every Jean-Claude vehicle is written. 'The Fight' serves two purposes: to prove that Jean-Claude is a proper action hero, and to give him a chance to show off his body. Like every self-made man, Jean-Claude is very proud of his body. 'It is important to have everything balanced', he is fond of stressing. 'I never made myself as big as some body-builders. There always has to be a sense of beauty, of proportion. I was always shaping the body, like a sculptor.'

There is one part of his body that Jean-Claude is especially proud of: his butt. This explains why, at the heart of every great Jean-Claude performance you will find 'The Butt Shot': a loving, lingering view of his bared ass in all its glory. And why begrudge him the indulgence? When all is said and done, it's the sort of butt you could spend many happy hours quietly contemplating, the sort of butt you could serve drinks off. It is, in Jean-Claude's own words, 'a very up, strong butt'.

I hate to have to end on a bum note, but it seems to me that something has dropped out of Jean-Claude's performances since he left the security of STV. The last truly enjoyable film he made was the transitional *Universal Soldier*. A happy blend of high camp and conspicuous homoerotica pumped up as hard action, *Universal Soldier* proved once again that Jean-Claude was at his best when acting dumb. Since then, he's been busy trying to prove he's more than just a hard-ass. He's got it into his head that he wants to be a serious actor. He's taken to wearing wire-rimmed spectacles during interviews. And he's become rather shy about giving his backside a chance.

Promoted as a *Shane* for the 1990s, with Jean-Claude as a latter-day Alan Ladd, *Nowhere to Run* is basically one long advert for *Families Need Fathers*, and about as interesting. *Hard Target*, directed by top-grossing Hong Kong action director John Woo, is a cynical concoction of artfully 'ironic' violence and painfully irritating, slow-motion photography. The plot pits Jean-Claude against a gang of thugs who sell kicks to men whose favourite sport is hunting down the city's down-and-outs. The script is littered with homophobic 'jokes' (favourite term of abuse: 'Tell that to your boyfriend'). It's all very anally retentive, without the erotic undercurrents that used to guarantee gay Jean-Claude watchers their shares of circumspect pleasures.

But that's not the worst crime. For this, the finger of accusation must point at Jean-Claude's hairdresser. Big kicks are all very well. Big hair is a major turn-off. And no butts.

The Boy Who Came Back

Interviews with Marc Almond, October/November 1994

OCTOBER 1994, and Marc Almond is back under the lights, trying a few things, seeing what works. Stripped to the waist, he looks fitter than you'd imagine – lean and muscular, with definition in all the right places. Fighting fit, in fact. As the camera clicks into action, he strikes a few poses with a fur stole, stifles a laugh and turns to the stylist: 'You don't think this looks too drag queeny, do you?'

Minutes later, he's skulking about in a fur coat, telling us about his trips to the dog races, doing his best to exude aggression. 'What are you going to call this piece?', he asks. 'Penis in Furs', I reply, and everyone laughs – him loudest of all. Finally, he drops the fur and tries some cock-rock posturing, strutting around the studio with an electric guitar – the one prop he specifically requested for the shoot. Really getting into the spirit of it, he runs his tongue across the guitar strings, parodying the antics of one of his greatest idols: Ziggy played guitar.

Marc Almond has undergone quite a few changes lately – not all to do with powder, paint and good lighting. For one thing, he's changed record labels – again. After a brief stint with WEA, he's now back with Phonogram, the people he parted company with over a decade ago, when Soft Cell were busily demonstrating the art of falling apart. (It's different now, he insists. This time around, they know exactly what they're dealing with.)

But there's more to it than that. This is the third time I've interviewed Almond, and the man happily sipping tea with me while the lights are being reset is a far cry from the jittery, tongue-tied creature I first encountered three years ago in the offices of WEA. Back then, he seemed worn out and wary – of himself as much as anybody else. Today, he's bright-eyed and visibly self-possessed. And he has rather a lot to say for himself.

'I look back on my time at WEA as the wilderness years', he announces, as I delve deep into my bag for my tape recorder. 'They started off with so much promise, but soon I came to realize that nothing I could do was right. I felt that I was at a creative peak, writing all these songs which were really heartfelt. They were true Marc Almond songs, if you like, but WEA didn't like them. They said they were "too Marc Almond". It was a case of, "No, we really think you should do something more radical and different." In other words, "so radical and so different it's no longer you." Everything I did was wrong. My confidence was completely shattered during my time at WEA. The chairman even turned around and told me that nobody wanted to listen to Marc Almond songs any more, so I'd better shape up my ideas.

'I do think it's important to always do something a bit different with each album. As an artist, you've always got to present a different facet of yourself, surprise people, even shock people sometimes. But people still have to be able to link it with you. I think it turns people off if they can't find me in the record.'

This was certainly true of *Tenement Symphony* – Almond's only studio album for WEA, one half of which was produced by Trevor Horn. The sleeve may have promised equal portions of 'Grit and Glitter', but for many of Almond's most ardent admirers it was a case of too much of one and not nearly enough of the other. 'The album was a complete disaster, basically', he admits now. 'Even though it had three singles ["Jackie", "The Days of Pearly Spencer" and "My Hand Over My Heart"], all of which got a fair amount of airplay, the whole look and feel of the album was wrong, right down to the picture on the cover. WEA insisted that I wear a tuxedo and make myself more presentable. I remember thinking, "who is this person on the cover of my record?"

'I realize now that it alienated a lot of my fan-base. I know a lot of people felt that my heart wasn't in it, and in a way they were right. It was a totally manufactured record – great slabs of kitsch which were all wonderful and fabulous just so long as you didn't mind the fact that you couldn't find me in them. Creatively speaking, *Tenement Symphony* was a completely barren experience for me. Especially with the whole Trevor Horn thing, basically I became a guest on my own record. And then of course I had to promote something I didn't believe in. For me, that was very depressing. It led to a lot of other problems, which I'd rather not talk about here. Last year was one of the worst years of my life. It was extremely traumatic. I really was driven to the brink . . . '

He pauses, promising to divulge the rest of the story on Monday, which is the day set aside for the interview. 'I'll play you some material from the new record then as well', he says. 'There's a lot of anger coming out of the stuff I've been doing lately which will need some explaining. Let's just say it's the first genuine thing I've done in a long time.'

Exactly a month later, I arrive at Marc Almond's Fulham address eager to pick up on our conversation, but mostly relieved that, after a string of cancelled appointments, the interview is finally about to take place. First there was some disagreement over the terms of the new record deal, then he had to rush off to New York, where the new album was being mixed.

In the intervening weeks, I've had plenty of time to reflect on a remark made by a friend, that Marc Almond experiences trauma the way most people experience blocked pores. Wasn't 'This Last Night In Sodom' supposed to be a record of the worst year of his life? And 'Torment And Toreros'? And 'Mother Fist'? Who is to say that whatever it is he wants to talk about today isn't something we've all heard about a dozen times before?

I'm also reminded of a comment he made the last time I interviewed him. 'I'm very aware of the fact that I can be a bit of a tragedy queen', he acknowledged. 'If there's not a tragedy there, I'll go ahead and create one.'

So here I am, standing outside what looks like an abandoned church, praying that Marc Almond is at home and hasn't legged it off to some remote part of the globe. I press the buzzer and within moments he's there, ushering me in with the offer of a cup of tea and a word of warning about the packing crates cluttering up the entrance hall. The place was a complete mess when he moved in, he explains – rubble everywhere. A year later, there's still a lot of work to be done.

I navigate my way into the living room, which is enormous. High above the door, the daylight gleams through stained-glass windows. The fireplace is bigger than my bathroom. A fur rug is spread out in front of the fire. Placed next to it, and dotted all around the room, are hordes of religious icons, giant crucifixes, burning candles. 'My candle burns at both ends', I think to myself, but say nothing except, 'this is very Marc Almond'.

It is also, I am about to discover, a very appropriate setting for the conversation which follows. He offers to play me some of the material rejected by WEA, and I listen appreciatively, posing a few questions here and there, remarking on how much better – how much darker – this stuff is than most of what ended up on *Tenement Symphony*. Evidently, this is precisely what he has been waiting to hear. Before very long, what began as a straightforward interview situation has evolved into something resembling a confessional. We're just coming to the end of a song called 'Looking For Love In All The Wrong Places' when Marc leaps up from the floor, switches the tape player off and perches himself on the coffee table next to me.

'There's a very addictive theme to a lot of these songs', he says. 'Addiction. Obsession. Compulsion. These have always been the themes to my songs, because these are the themes to my life in a way. I've always been an addict. I've always had problems with drink, drugs, sex – all those things. Part of the reason why it all became so terrible last year was that I had to face up to the fact that I had a really bad problem with sleeping pills and Valium. I'd been addicted to Valium for twelve years, and to Halcyon sleeping pills for twelve years. I'd been through other addictions – I'd been addicted to just about every other drug at some point or another – but this was the worst. When they banned Halcyon in Britain, because people were going psycho on them, I travelled abroad to get supplies of the pills. I had a doctor in America, a doctor in Thailand. My life was completely controlled by pills. The drugs brought me to my knees.'

Looking back, he reckons the problem is rooted in his child-hood ('it stems from abuse', he says, quite matter-of-factly), but only began to manifest itself around 1982, shortly after his career with Soft Cell took off. Success had a lot to do with it, he says. 'Success gives you a licence to feed your addictions. It gives you the money and the power to indulge yourself. And the demands of success are so enormous. I started taking numbing pills to help me cope with the pressure, and before I knew where I was they were adding to the problem. Of course I never realized that there was a problem.

Everyone around me told me for years that I had a problem, but I couldn't see it. The drugs were affecting my judgement. I became agrophobic. That's why the concerts became so few and far between, because I just couldn't get it together. Huge chunks of my memory were being wiped out. I'd have conversations with people, and forget them the next day. I'd forget appointments. I'd forget the words to songs. Doing the Albert Hall show was a terribly traumatic experience. People who've seen me in concert over the years will know that I often forget the words to songs, and have to start again, or scrap the song altogether. Of course I didn't associate this with the drugs at the time.'

In retrospect, he claims that one of the reasons he allowed himself to be so manipulated over the *Tenement Symphony* album was that he simply didn't have the strength to stand up for himself. 'I love "Jackie", and I adore "My Hand Over My Heart". But it didn't all add up. At that time I really needed a lifting experience. It didn't lift me. I felt that I'd compromised, sold out. There were songs I really needed to get out at that time, songs that expressed how I was feeling and what I was going through, and they were dropped or relegated to B sides. And I didn't have it in me to fight back. So life became completely abusive – whether it was me being abused, me abusing myself, or me abusing other people. I became attracted to people who were abusive to me. I became a freak magnet, attracting people who were as messed up as I was. I've always had a bit of a Mother Teresa complex anyway, but it got completely out of hand. I lost all confidence in music. I lost all interest in standing up to the record company. It was anything for a quiet life, really.'

Only it didn't stay that way. In the run up to Christmas 1993, he was pushed to the brink – literally – when a couple of his new-found friends decided to throw him over a sixth-floor balcony. 'Luckily for me, the police arrived just in time. I was unconscious on the floor, and quite badly scarred. I don't want to sensationalize it too much, but it was a turning point.' Within weeks, he'd checked into a drug rehabilitation clinic, paid for by WEA. 'They took a photo of me when I arrived, with my face all bloated. I was heading for latter-day Elvis.' The regimen was strict, he says – up at 7.30 every morning, scrubbing floors, followed by hours of group therapy. 'You weren't ever allowed to be on your own. You had to be with somebody every minute of the day. It was tough, but I got a lot from it. It cleared my head out. I became calmer, more collected.'

After two months, he was driven out of rehab by the arrival of the *Sun* newspaper. 'I made a dramatic exit in a blacked-out limousine', he recalls, laughing. 'Within three days, I was back in New York working on the album, still withdrawing. I'm still going through withdrawal even now. The hardest things to cope with are the waking nightmares. It's like all the doors in your mind have been shut off for years and years. All the dreams that you should have had are locked behind those doors, so when you come off the drugs and your mind is unlocked, you get waking dreams, hallucinations and things. People talk about withdrawing from heroin, but prescription pills are very, very nasty. Believe me, withdrawing from twelve years of Valium and sleeping pills is a terrifying experience. There were times when I thought the trees were coming alive to get me.'

And what now? Does he consider himself fully cured? 'I'm not saying I'm cured exactly', he says, choosing his words carefully. 'I'll always be an addictive person. But I think I've learned how to cope with it. I know that if I am tempted to do drugs, it'll end up in a binge. Nowadays, if somebody offers me a line of coke, I say no. Not because I don't want the coke, but because I want the whole fucking gramme. And it won't stop there. Next it'll be two grammes. Then it'll be me ringing someone up at three o'clock in the morning for a third gramme.'

> 'I only do it for the madness'
> 'What kind of madness, Marc?'
> 'Rock and roll madness'
> (Interview with Marc Bolan, 1972)

Marc Almond has been going back to his roots. 'It's a very kind of punky, rock and roll, fuck off album in a way', he says, sorting through a pile of tapes, lining up a few more tracks for me. 'Of all the ways it could have gone, that's the way it ended up. And I'm sort of glad really. I went to New York to get away from what was happening in London, and the album has got that feeling in a way. It's not an album about New York, but it's got that kind of dirt under the fingernails feel to it. It was time to throw out all the sequinned outfits, and get back into some leather. It was very necessary for me, after the experiences of the last few years, to come back with something that says, "I'm awake. I've been asleep for ten years, but now I'm awake." I suppose if you want to think of any album in the past, it echoes back to "This Last Night In Sodom".'

He starts the first track ('It's called "Lie" and it's all about a sick relationship'), and it suddenly strikes me that he is only half right. If you had to find a reference point in Marc Almond's personal back-catalogue, then 'This Last Night in Sodom' would probably be it. But in actual fact the tough, sinewy sound booming out of the speakers echoes a lot further back than that – way, way back to the people and the sounds he grew up with: Ziggy, T Rex, the Velvets, the New York Dolls. There are even contributions from singing Doll David Johannson and ex-Velvet John Cale.

He's absolutely right about one thing, though. On the evidence of the five or six tracks he plays me, this is an album which leaves you in little doubt that his eyes are open. It's by far and away the best thing he's done in years. And it's very, very druggy, with titles like 'Addicted' and lyrics comparing obsessive love affairs to drug dependency. He says he found it ironic that WEA didn't want him to record these songs, choosing instead to push him into making dance music – that is, music for people to take drugs to. 'Especially nowadays, when you have bands like Suede singing about the Ecstasy experience, and the heroin experience. I mean, the things I write about aren't that dissimilar to the things he writes about, so how come I'm finding myself being suppressed and he's not? I started to think, is it to do with homophobia? Is it because I'm a gay man? As a gay man, I'm not supposed to talk about those experiences. I suspect that it would all have been rather different if I'd had a girlfriend in tow. Then they would have been happy for me to share my experiences of drugs. Or of gay sex.'

The final track he plays me is called 'The Idol'. It's a song about the kinds of stars who took it all too far, went for overkill, burned themselves out in the name of fame. They're all there: Judy, Jimmy, Elvis, Bolan – right up to and including Kurt Cobain. 'I've always enjoyed writing about stars and icons,' says Marc, 'whether it's the aspirations of "The Stars We Are" or something like "Saint Judy", which is about the crumbling of an icon. I've always been fascinated by the way we project our hopes, our dreams and even our failings on to them.'

The song opens with what Marc himself describes as 'the most blatant rip-off of the intro to "Jean Genie" ever heard.' About half way through, just after the adoring crowd has changed its tune, and started proclaiming hate instead of love, there is the unmistakable sound of a car crashing into a tree. A reference to the death of Marc Bolan, obviously, but one that also incorporates a sample from the intro to 'Tainted Love'. What's this, I wonder, a reference to his own rock and roll suicide?

Marc Almond laughs. 'I suppose what I'm saying is that all idols will let you down if you expect too much of them – including me. I always hate it when people write to me saying I'm their idol. I can never be anything but a let down. So it's a jokey reference to my own idol status. I don't really think of myself as being in the same league as the people I'm singing about, but I've had a taste of what that kind of success has to offer. If there's one thing I've learned, it's that there is always somebody ready to say that you're washed up, that you're finished. And all you can really do in that situation is do your best to ensure that you bounce back again.'

And with that, he turns the tape player off and offers to make me another cup of tea. Now that's what I call a star, boys. That's what I call a star.

Richard Loves Cindy

GAY film critic Richard Dyer tells an amusing anecdote about how he was once outed by one of his students during a lecture on feminist film theory. Evidently bored by all this talk about semiotics, psychoanalysis and the complex terms of identification, the student asked a very simple, very direct question: Was 'sir' gay or not? 'Yes', Dyer replied, but why had the student suspected as much? Which visible sign of his gayness had given him away? Was it the tone of his voice? The cut of his hair? The fact that he had once written a book called '*Gays and Film*'?

Actually, it was none of these. It was simply his use of the word 'heterosexual'. As this keen student of human nature had observed, heterosexuals tend not to use this word, mainly because they rarely have cause to think of themselves as possessing a sexual orientation at all.

Of course I have no idea what bearing, if any, this lesson has on the recent anouncement by Richard Gere and Cindy Crawford that they are, in fact, both heterosexual and happily married. In May 1994, in the same week that 200,000 men, women and children were slaughtered in Rwanda, South Africa held its first democratic elections, 64 per cent of American voters expressed little or no confidence in President Clinton and the Tories came a cropper in the local government elections, these glamorous champions in the struggle for world peace and all-round niceness took out a full-page ad in *The Times* newspaper, at an estimated cost of £20,000. Richard and Cindy's 'personal statement' was writ large to assure their friends and fans that 'we got married because we love each other'; that 'we are heterosexual and monogamous'; that 'there is not and never has been a pre-nuptial agreement of any kind'; that 'there are no plans, nor have there ever been any plans for a divorce'; that in spite of rumours to the contrary, 'we remain very married'.

Speaking as someone with little faith and less interest in the state of holy matrimony, I must confess that I have no concept of what being 'very married' actually means. Can the quality of a marriage be measured according to the amount of time a couple spend together, by the size and quantity of gifts they lavish upon one another, on the degree of love and respect they display for each other and the cameras? Call me old fashioned, but it seems to me that one is either married or one is not.

What I do find illuminating about Richard and Cindy's announcement is the fact that they felt they had to make it at all. Certainly, rumours of deviation from the enshrined heterosexual state of marriage never appear to have bothered either of them much in the past. Less than a year before they placed their ad, Cindy was caught cavorting with k.d. lang on the cover of '*Vanity Fair*', in a pose that precipitated a thousand articles on 'lesbian chic'. The following January, Richard told the same magazine in no mean terms that the question of whether he was actually gay or straight was nobody's business but his own (though, presumably, what he really meant to say was that it was nobody's business but his and Cindy's). 'The accusation is meaningless', he said at the time. 'This kind of silly prejudice cripples everyone . . . It's insane. It's school-yard stuff, real kid's stuff. But if you start to take a defensive mode and say, 'No, I'm not', it gives credence to the idea that there's something wrong with it. I have no interest in putting myself in that category.'

Which must have made the decision to call up the *Times* ad department a real conflict of interests. If saying 'I'm not' lends credence to the notion that saying 'I am' is somehow morally reprehensible, then saying 'I'm not' over and over again in letters an inch high must really force a space between what is right and what is wrong. So what prompted the decision? The *Times* ad draws atten-tion to a 'a very crude, ignorant and libellous article in a French tabloid' (called *Voici*, in case anyone wants to order a back copy – though they've probably all gone by now). Since the publication of said article, Richard and Cindy go on to say, speculation seems to have reached 'some sort of critical mass' (whatever that means). The ad concludes with the couple confirming that they will continue to support 'difficult' causes (including 'AIDS research and treatment' and 'Gay and Lesbian Rights'), and asking journalists to kindly remember that 'marriage is hard enough without all this negative speculation', and that 'thoughts and words are very powerful'.

Indeed they are. Which rather begs the question of why two people apparently so committed to the promotion of lesbian and gay equality should release a statement which helps reinforce the idea that to be labelled lesbian or gay amounts to a negative slur. It's not even as if such statements have the desired effect. As poor old Jason Donovan learned too late, telling the world that you are not gay doesn't stop people from speculating that you might not be entirely straight; all it really does is confirm that you are somebody who wants to be seen as being anything but gay.

So let's hear it for Richard and Cindy, the perfectly not-gay couple. They may have changed their plans somewhat, now that they have officially split and all, but their names will be for ever joined as two people who went to extraordinary lengths to set the record straight, only to end up communicating a mixed message. Or something.

Ring My Bell

Interview with Andy Bell, May 1994

THE first time I met Andy Bell, we were in a hotel room in Manchester. Slightly tacky and thoroughly gauche, the Britannia Hotel seemed as good a place as any to ponder the pop art invention that is Erasure. We met on the eve of their last tour, the one that recently came out on video, the one where Andy exposed his not-especially-pert buttocks, danced around like a teenage girl at her first school disco, and dedicated a cover version of 'Somewhere Over The Rainbow' to 'all the beautiful people who have died of AIDS!' – all in the same spirit of 'Hey, let's put on a show!' that so moved the young Judy Garland and Mickey Rooney in all those MGM musicals they did together. That, ladies and gentlemen, is the essence of Erasure – the sense that it's all just a bit of fun really, and if anyone happens to make a bit of money or widen the horizons of a few anally retentive homophobes into the bargain, well good luck to them, but let's not forget what we're here for.

And they haven't, god bless them. Calling their greatest hits album *Pop! The First Twenty Hits* was a gamble, but one that will probably pay off. After nine years in the business of making bright, sparkling, soaraway pop singles, Erasure's bubble shows no signs of bursting – *Pop 2! The Next Twenty Hits* isn't such an unlikely prospect. And the reason for this is quite simply that Erasure are purveyors of pop music at its purest and most durable – people who instinctively know that a good pop song isn't judged on what it makes you think, but on how it makes you feel. Face it, they're fabulous at it. Who cares what lyrics like 'And they covered up the sun / Until the birds had flown away / And the fishes in the sea had gone to sleep' read like on paper? On record they sound twice as impassioned and – yes – just as 'meaningful' as anything engineered by the Pet Shop Boys. When critics dismiss Erasure as mind-numbingly boring electro-tarts, all they're really doing is running away from the fact that pop – despite the efforts of pop-analysts to persuade us otherwise – is essentially an emotional, rather than a cerebral medium.

61: *Ring My Bell*

All of which needs saying, none of which makes the task of interviewing Andy Bell any easier. The last time we met, we got on fairly well, or so I thought. Certainly I went off and wrote what I took to be a pretty favourable piece. Andy remembers it, or at least he remembers me. As I take my seat in a hired room at the Kensington Gore Hotel, he asks me how I am, what clubs I've been going to, and so on. No stranger to this situation, he is none the less palpably, excruciatingly nervous. He tells me how Garland once slept in this room, on the very bed where he has just finished posing awkwardly for the photographer. He suggests that maybe this explains why the bed is so wonky. 'It's called the Venus Suite', he says. And then, after a deadly pause: 'She didn't die here, did she?'

'I don't think so', I tell him, realizing of course that all this talk about my social life and Judy Garland's anti-social death is simply a way of putting off what we've really come to talk about: Andy Bell. For the life of me I can't work what it is that is unsettling him. I start to entertain the idea that this isn't really the flamboyant singing half of Erasure seated on the floor in front of me at all, but an imposter who lives in fear of being found out. That's the thing about Andy Bell, you see. Off-stage, he doesn't look or act the least bit like a pop star. Imagine, if you will, that you'd never even heard of Erasure. You walk into a room full of people and there, sitting quietly in the corner, is Andy Bell. Now imagine that somebody offers to pay you a million quid if you can just point to the person most likely to enjoy larking about in rubber leotards. You would never see that million. Andy Bell is the last person you would point to. He is, as somebody once remarked of Rock Hudson, the last guy you'd have figured.

Not that he doesn't at times feel hampered by his celebrity. By way of an ice-breaker, I ask him what he made of the vote to lower the gay age of consent. He lights a cigarette, says he relishes the fact that gay sex was made legal at eighteen under a Tory government, and would have been well and truly shocked had it been dropped any lower. 'But to be honest with you, I've not really been switched on with those things. It all seems a bit surreal to me, really. Even when I do go along on a march or something, I don't feel as if I'm a part of it all. I always feel like I'm on my own. It's something about not being able to let go, anywhere. I can't imagine myself ever really letting go. Unless I'm really out of it, I can't get into things. And I'm always scared when people start shouting and that. I'm terrified of being arrested. I always think it would be like that film with Brad Davis, *Midnight Express*. I always imagine myself being the only gay person in jail, and being raped all the time and stuff. I'd have to have my own little wing.'

On the face of it, Andy Bell appears to have done a lot of growing up in public. Despite this, he's still the baby of the class, the one who always sat at the back, dreading the moment when teacher would single him out to answer a really difficult question. 'You're quite shy, really, aren't you?' I say, none too tactfully.

'Yes', he answers. There is a long pause, during which I consider the remote possibility that one reason for his shyness might be the habit other people – journalists especially – have of drawing attention to it.

I push a little further. 'I suppose it's that old story about introverted people letting the repressed side of themselves out on stage.'

'Yes', he says again.

I'm beginning to wish I had never set off on this line of questioning when, out of the blue, Andy Bell introduces a new one all of his own. 'This journalist asked me earlier whether I'd ever been for psychoanalysis', he says, stubbing out his cigarette. 'I told her, "no", but it's funny that she should have said that, isn't it?'

'Is it?', I say, not wanting to sound too sure either way.

'Yes, it is, 'cos recently I was in the Cockring in Amsterdam talking to this guy. I was really interested in him, 'cos he had rings in his nose and his ears and everywhere and I was wondering whether he had any rings anywhere else. So I was talking to him, and he just turned to me and said, "Have you ever been for psychoanalysis?" I suppose it must strike people as quite odd, the fact that I am always being asked my opinions on things, just because I'm a singer with a band. I mean, it's ridiculous really, isn't it? I wouldn't go for psychoanalysis, though. Just because somebody has passed an exam, why should they be more of an authority on how your mind works than you are? I'd end up a complete mess if I did it, I think. I'd start worrying about why I wore a certain outfit, why I said what I said, why I'm sitting on the floor now as I'm talking to you . . . '

63: *Ring My Bell*

He laughs. It is the sort of laugh people emit when they're not sure whether what they've just said was the right thing to say or not. I smile reassuringly. A smile is all that he has been waiting for. Without my even asking, Andy Bell divulges the fact that he has been having some pretty weird dreams lately. 'There's one in particular. It's a sort of recurring dream about a friend of mine who was ill. I'm on this train with my boyfriend and my best friend from school, this girl called Helen Adams. We get off the train and find out where this guy lives. We're kind of like going to all the old places we used to go, like toilets and bars and stuff, and leaving all this stuff, books and things, that had something to do with the relationship. Then we get to this guy's house. He is lying on the stairs and he is too weak to open the door. So we open the door and we go upstairs. There is a bundle of rags lying at the top of the stairs, and as we get near it, it opens its mouth and I realize that it's a sea lion. And then I wake up, 'cos I don't want to go on any further . . . '

Andy Bell is hard pushed to account for Erasure's extraordinary longevity. 'I suppose you could say it's because we're not very star-ish. I mean, we don't have managers and all that stuff. We deal with a lot of the every day running of things. We watch the budget. We don't believe in the trimmings. I suppose we're quite regular chaps really. People always expect you to be much more prima donna-ish than you are. Then they get very disappointed when you're not rude to them.'

But it can't only be a matter of balancing the books, surely. You need to actually make some money first, and that means selling records. And Erasure do sell records – lots of them. Is it not, I suggest, more a question of Andy and Vince never having generated the sort of pop hysteria that wears off after a year or two, leaving a stockpile of cheesy T-shirts where once there was the promise of a steady career? And surely the band's distinctive yet unashamedly derivative sound has something to do with it? Even at their best, Erasure have always sounded like a few of your favourite songs of a few years ago mixed together, have always sounded vaguely retro in spite of their up to-the-minute production. 'I think it's very modern, our stuff', Andy says, quietly but firmly. 'I mean, it doesn't really date, does it?'

Erasure recently released a new album. It's called *I Say, I Say, I Say*. The title is a reminder that, when all is said is done, Erasure are simply out to have a good laugh. The album itself is a reminder of every other album they've ever done: bright, bubbly, quite ravishing in places, and very, very serviceable. 'Always' was the perfect choice of single – not because, as Andy says, 'it's very Euro' or because 'if it was entered for Eurovision, it would win hands down', but because the title says it all really. It says dependable. It says consistent. It says for ever. Andy says it makes him think of a few things, too. 'It reminds me of Black, that song "Wonderful Life". And it reminds me of a track called "American Lover", which is a sort of gay classic song.'

'Always' was written in Amsterdam, along with another track called 'Blues Away'. As a record of their shared birthplace, they also share the same chord structure. The rest of the album was written all over the place. And in case anyone is wondering what it's all about, Andy would like to point out that, as is the case with most Erasure albums, 'a lot of the lyrics are really nonsensical. What happens is, we write a melody first, and then in order to remember a chorus I'll attach some words to it. More often than not, I can't think of any new words, so those words become the lyrics. You have to write the whole lyric around these words, and you don't usually know what the song means until about a year later. I never know what I'm singing about half the time. Never. Not until someone else tells me.'

By 'someone else' he means, presumably, 'some journalist'. Not that he has any real grievances with the press. As he is only too ready to acknowledge, Erasure's press relations have improved no end over the past couple of years. Even the tour, which afforded plenty of opportunities for putting the boot in, received rave reviews in places he expected to get slated. 'I was a bit surprised by the rock fraternity', Andy says. 'Usually they get very sniffy. There was a picture of me with my knickers and corset and Judy shoes in Q magazine, and a caption that just said, "Is this the future of rock?" I thought, "Well, if it was I'd be very pleased". The thing is, I think Erasure are very rock and roll. We're the most rock and roll you can get. We represent everything that people aren't supposed to like. Rock and roll has always been measured by its outrage factor. And

65: *Ring My Bell*

I don't just mean showing your bum and things like that. Erasure isn't in your face. It's up your nose, I think. I believe you should always make people smell the shit, really.'

If it has taken Erasure a little longer than most to earn the respect they undoubtedly deserve (and let's face it, asking people to stick their noses up your bum isn't exactly the surest method of broadening your fan base), pinpointing the precise moment when the world went pop is no mean feat either. Andy thinks the Abba thing probably helped a lot. 'One of the reasons I always compare us to them is that when they were around and were doing really well, people wouldn't admit to liking them. They knew all the words to the songs and everything, but only afterwards were people prepared to admit to liking them.'

'But that's the crucial difference between you and Abba', I say. 'With Abba the respect only came after they had disbanded.'

'Well, it happened during their demise as well.'

'But you're not in your demise. Are you?'

'No. I hope not, anyway.'

Not wanting to end on such a bum note, I ask Andy Bell what he made of Bjorn Again's reply to Erasure's 'Abba-esque' EP, the quaintly titled 'Erasure-ish'. 'I thought it was quite good', he says. 'I think it's a shame it didn't do better, really. I quite like Bjorn Again. When I first saw them I thought, "I can't take this." I was too big an Abba fan. But since they've been around I've sort of grown used to them and let them in slowly. One of the videos they did for that EP was with one of the guys in an outfit like one of mine, with tassles and things, and he was just prancing about and wiggling his bum. It was like a *Carry On* film, like a straight person imitating a gay person. But I can forgive them for that. It was a compliment really. It was tacky, but tacky is okay. In hindsight it's always a treasure.'

It Only Took a Minute ...

'SO the rumour is we're all gay now, are we?' says Jason (the sexy one).

'Am I gay?', asks Gary (the talented one). 'I am? . . . Oh good. Just as long as I know.'

'Does anyone think I'm gay?' asks Howard (the one with the small tattoo and the large packet).

'No. You're the only one people think is straight', says Jason.

'Why aren't I gay?' says Howard. 'What's wrong with me? . . . I want to be queer like you lot!'

Well he would say that, wouldn't he? *Take That – In Private* (Virgin Books, 1994) is the sort of book the boys say they've always wanted to do – 'honest, open and frank', 'raw, uncut and above all revealing'. According to the opening blurb, 'there's stuff in here about us that we didn't even realize ourselves'. Presumably this doesn't include author Alex Kadis's observation that Mark (the pretty one, the one all the girls fancy) is 'a real animal lover', or that Robbie (the funny one, the one all the boys fancy) is the 'most stridently heterosexual of men'. But we get the picture. This is Take That 'As We've Never Seen Them Before'. This is Take That 'As They Really Are'. This is Take That 'For the Fans'.

Like most sensible people, I became a Take That fan only when it became absolutely necessary. I know it's marginally less uncool to say that you liked them before they crossed over from the gay clubs to the tabloids, that they were somehow more 'authentic' when they still 'belonged to us'. But there you go. Authenticity has never been a good measure of great pop, and the fact is, Take That have got better the further they've strayed from their northern gay roots. Their early videos may have featured the boys larking about in bondage gear and having jam and jelly rubbed into their naughty bits, but there was still something distinctly cheesy about them. (In December 1993, Howard confessed to *The Face* that there was jam under his foreskin 'for weeks' after filming.)

Then everything changed. When their first three singles ('Do What You Like', 'Promises', 'Once You've Tasted Love') all failed to whet enough teenage appetites, Take That did the smart thing and cleaned up. Out went the leather jockstraps and beats that stank of stale poppers; in came a more flexible dress code and a breezier, brassier sound. Aided by a video that showed five normal, healthy boys enjoying all the fun of the boxing ring, 'It Only Takes A Minute' (their first cover version, a spit in the eye of 'authenticity' if ever there was one) entered the British chart at number twenty-five. Take That were on course for what pop pundits love to refer to as 'world domination'.

But it wasn't until the release of 'Could It Be Magic' that this worldly listener finally surrendered to their charms. In theory, it should never have worked – we are talking about a cover of an old Barry Manilow number, after all. But something about the arrangement, and the fact that Robbie (cheeky, chirpy and irrepressibly cocky) had replaced Gary (soulful, earnest and painfully dull) on lead vocals, meant that this song came across in a way that previous solicitations hadn't. It promised that everything could be magic, if only for a minute or three. So when Robbie and the boys sang a chorus of 'Come into my arms' and 'Take me', it seemed churlish to resist.

Plus there was the video, of course. Egos far greater than mine have tripped out over the orgiastic excesses of this near-perfect pop promo. Julie Burchill, enthusing wildly in *The Modern Review*, compared it to 'a Bruce Weber spermfest', before focusing on the 'three girls in their best Top Shop finery', hanging around the television studio where our five heroes have taken to strutting their spunky stuff. 'More pungently than any sniggering indie hymn to E', she wrote, 'this video captures beautifully the blurring of the line between affection and attraction, between boy and girl and boy.'

It's probably just a question of perspective (I'm a gay man and Julie Burchill, for all that she'd like to be, isn't), but the girls she speaks of barely enter into my view of things. The only line I see being blurred is the line between commercial circumspection and rampant homoeroticism. The sexual energy is the energy that is invariably unleashed when boys are encouraged to hang out together. The girls, bless them, are simply hovering on the sidelines. They may be inside the same studio, but really they are no different to thousands of Take That fans, oozing with desire while their noses stay firmly pressed against the glass.

'We don't mind the rumours about being gay', Robbie was quoted as saying recently. 'One of us might even be gay.' Personally, I don't really care whether there is any truth to the rumours or not. If any members of the band are gay, then they should be commended for having managed to avoid publicly confirming the fact without resorting to the sorts of homophobic denials which are part and parcel of the pop closet. Take That are living proof that you can take the boys out of the gay clubs, but you needn't necessarily take the gay clubs out of the boys. And clever boys that they are, they seem to like it that way.

Think, for a moment, of Jason Donovan (only for a moment, I promise), and the difference is clear. And abundantly queer. When *The Face* ran an article suggesting that Donovan might not be all he seemed, he sued on account of what his lawyer described as 'a poisonous slur'. Asked by the same magazine how he felt about lads shouting 'faggot' at him in the street, Mark Owen was unfazed: 'I blow them a kiss.'

And if they aren't really gay? Well, I suppose the worst you could say of them is that their promises never mean anything they make they seem. But really, isn't that what all great pop is about? Take That's gay pose (if that's all it is) is no more cynical than Brett Anderson claiming to be a bisexual who has never had a homosexual experience. And a lot more fun. At least they've never laid claim to being anything more than a bunch of pop tarts.

How long the fun will last is anybody's guess. Popular wisdom has it that, as in the case of every bubble-gum band from the Osmonds to Bros, Take That's bubble will soon burst. And what will poor Robbie do then, poor thing? Odds are, he'll become a children's television presenter. Gary will go solo, quickly mutating into George Michael without the beard. Mark will find a nice girl and settle down. And Jason and Howard will go back to dancing on crap music programmes like *The Hitman and Her*.

But let's pray it isn't over yet. They may have danced about in some pretty dodgy items of clothing (Howard's sarong and Gary's unflattering lycra vests spring immediately to mind). They may have made some even dodgier associations (I know we gay folks are meant to look up to her as a survivor and all that, but to me Lulu will always be that short-arse who sang 'Shout'). Still Take That are about as important as pop ever gets. Better than anyone, they have demonstrated that you can have a brilliant career as an object of teenage girls' fantasies and still spare a thought for the boys. While it may be a little rash to suggest that, in the big, bad homophobic world of pop, everything changes, Take That give us reason to believe that, occasionally, some things do.

Oh, Donna

ONCE we had a girl. Donna was her name. And we loved our girl. We loved her like no other. And then, just when we needed her most, she turned her back on us. At least that's how the story went.

There is a scene in Mark Christopher's short film *The Dead Boys' Club* which pretty much sums up gay relationships with Donna Summer. A gay man has just died of AIDS, and his lover and a friend – both aged around forty, both survivors of the disco generation – are sorting through his belongings, dividing up piles of clothes, books and records. Hovering in the background, and barely able to disguise his discomfort, is a younger gay man in his early twenties.

'What about the albums?' the dead man's lover asks. To which his friend replies: 'You can have the Smiths and the disco greats, but the Donna Summer is all mine.'

The younger man looks shocked. 'Donna Summer?' he asks, as the friend selects an album and hugs it to his chest.

The older queen is unfazed. Smiling knowingly, he turns to his accuser and waggles a finger: 'Your generation will never know what you missed.'

Do you remember the 1970s? Donna Summer does – kind of. She remembers that 'everybody was partying, and dressing like maniacs'. She remembers that 'They had afros and, god knows, high heels, pump heels, stack heels and bell bottoms – you name it.' She remembers that, for an awful lot of people, 'It was just a very wild time.'

But she doesn't remember ever having been a part of it. Not really. Not in the way most people were a part of it. Not in the sense of people happily dancing and fucking their brains out. The way Donna Summer remembers the 1970s, 'It was right about the time that I started to become successful. Because of my job, because of my responsibilities, because I was always in the process of travelling, I think I missed out on a lot of things. I didn't experience it for myself in some ways.'

If this is true (and I've been warned that Ms Summer takes a dim view of anybody who says things which aren't true), then you have to credit her with having made a pretty good show of things at the time. The way I remember Donna Summer, she was the embodiment of all that that most excessive of decades had to offer. This is the woman, remember, who came to fame on the back of a seventeen-minute orgasm of a song entitled 'Love To Love You Baby'. And I do mean 'on the back of'. Her press notes remind us that 'Summer ad-libbed a vocal pattern over a pulsating, erotic techno-groove while lying on her back on the studio floor with the lights dimmed.'

She has since claimed that she never intended to record that particular song; that it was thrust upon her; that it was the result of a few hours messing about in the studio; that it didn't represent who she was; that all that heavy breathing simply wasn't her. The songs that followed suggest otherwise: 'I Feel Love', 'Hot Stuff', 'Bad Girls' – lusty, gutsy songs about female sexuality and self-determination, sung by a woman whose role as an upfront diva empowered her to say all those things women simply aren't supposed to say: 'Friday night, and the strip is hot'; 'how's about some hot stuff, baby, this evening?'; 'she works hard for the money, so you'd better treat her right'.

And didn't we ever. For years, Summer was the undisputed Queen of Gay Disco. Gay men took her to their hearts and paid her their money, not only because she dared to sing about the pleasures of being bad, but because she invited us to form a bond with her, to experience those pleasures as she experienced them. 'Now you and me, we're both the same', she sang on 'Bad Girls'. 'But you call yourself by a different name.'

Nowadays, Donna Summer 'feels love' rather differently. Gone are the times when she used to lie back and think of the next twelve-inch. Gone too is the woman who made her acting debut as the disco-dancing star of *Thank God It's Friday* – possibly one of the worst movies of all time, amounting to little more than a cynical attempt to beat *Saturday Night Fever* to the box office receipts. The new, reformed Donna Summer still likes to keep abreast of what's happening on the dance scene, but these days Friday nights are for the family. She says her perspective on life has changed considerably over the years, that she is 'probably more reflective' now.

'I don't see myself as only being here to enjoy myself', she explains. 'I don't see happiness as the only virtue in life. I see now that routine and sometimes sorrow helps build character. If somebody has suffered something and they sing a song, then they bring something to that song which they couldn't have brought to it if they hadn't suffered. And I do find that, even in myself, there is more sensitivity to the things I see than I used to have. I think there's been a lot of emotional, spiritual, I don't know, *soulful*, growth in me. I think I love people with a different kind of love. I see them a lot more empathetically.'

What the exact nature of Donna Summer's suffering is I really couldn't tell you. She talks a lot about 'the confusion' which entered her life some time around the early 1980s, shortly before God came along and put her straight. The woman who once believed in mirror-balls is now guided by a higher light. She describes her relationship with God as 'very personal', which seems to indicate that I shouldn't push her on the subject. I don't, but like most born-again Christians she can't resist an invitation to let another living person share in the joy she has known. 'I was at probably one of the lowest points in my life', she says, preparing me for the precise moment at which the spirit touched her. 'Had I not had God with me facing the confusion in my life at that point, I probably would have hurt myself. After a lot of these personal things happened in my life, I would not have had the spiritual, the emotional or the physical stamina to overcome anything. And I know now that having that to fall back on was certainly the foundation of my being able to overcome. And I'm very thankful for that. It's something I couldn't imagine living without. It's the most important thing in my life, so far as my sanity and my sense of balance is concerned.'

It was shortly after Donna Summer made her peace with God that she was alleged to have made the remarks which drove an almighty great wedge between her and her most loyal fans. Reports began filtering through to the gay press, claiming that Summer had said that gay men were 'sinners' and that AIDS was 'a divine ruling'. The story did the rounds, before being picked up by *New York* magazine, which published an article on 5 August 1991, repeating the previous allegations and also referring to a song written for

Summer by her longtime collaborator, the late Paul Jabara (the man responsible for such hits as 'Last Dance' and 'Enough Is Enough', who died of AIDS that same year). According to *New York*, the song, entitled 'We're Gonna Make It', had been dropped from Summer's 1991 album *Mistaken Identity* on the basis that it 'would serve as an apology' to the gay community.

At this point, Summer filed a $25 million libel suit, claiming that the story was 'completely false' and that it had caused 'serious damage' to her career. 'The article in *New York* magazine hurts me deeply', she was quoted as saying at the time. 'It also hurts those people who read the article and believe it to be true.' Months before his death, Summer served Jabara with a subpoena relating to her lawsuit. He died before the case was settled.

Naturally, I'm interested in knowing what the outcome of the libel suit was. Curiously, Donna Summer has no intention of telling me. 'Let me just say this', she says, sounding seriously pissed off. 'I'm not at liberty to talk about any of that stuff. I'm only at liberty to say this one thing, that it was settled amicably. Both parties were pleased at the outcome. I'm not supposed to talk about it publicly, so I really can't make any statement whatsoever. I mean, I will be . . . so, I mean, let's put it like this . . . No, I really can't talk about it. It's almost impossible to say anything without saying something and getting into a whole other lawsuit about something different. The lawsuit ended itself amicably.'

But surely the whole point of the suit was to clear her name, I protest. Where's the sense in not talking about it? Surely she only entered into the whole thing so that she could prove her innocence once and for all? 'Absolutely. I got tired of, y'know, magazines writing things that weren't true. I felt like it was too high a profile a magazine to let it rest, and so I went after that one. I mean, it wasn't the first time, but it was the first one that I felt was so high profile that in some ways it was gonna damage myself. So, let us end the conversation at that.'

And we do, more or less. Realizing that there's little point in pursuing this particular line of questioning, I ask Donna Summer what she thinks about Madonna. 'Nothing', she says, tetchily. 'I don't think about her. I mean, she's there. I don't buy her records. She's not the kind of artist I'm interested in. I'm more into singers like Whitney Houston, or people of that genre. I'm not so into what Madonna does as a professional. That's not making any criticism of her, whether she's good or bad. I'm told she works very hard at what she does.'

The reason I'm asking, I explain, is that she seems to occupy the same space that you once did. Madonna is very much the gay diva of the moment, the 1990s Bad Girl to your 1970s Bad Girl. And yes, I believe she does work hard for the money. 'I don't really think about it', Donna Summer says in a voice which suggests she'd much rather be talking about something else. 'I mean, I'm not trying to evade anything. I just don't give it much thought.'

I invite Donna Summer to give me a taste of what she does think about, what her goals are, where she intends to go from here. 'I just want to be free to be who I am,' she says, 'and not biased by other people's opinions of the past, future or present. I just wanna be who I am – whatever that means, wherever that is right now, or at some time in the future. I want to be allowed to grow at my own pace, and do all the things that I feel it is necessary for me to do. I wanna be all that I can be, whether that's an actress, a singer, or a dancer, or a writer, or a painter. I don't wanna be limited. I refuse to be limited. And if somebody tries to limit me, I will find a way to express myself.'

Taking this as some kind of warning not to fence her in, I ask Donna Summer whether there is anything else she wants to say. 'Not really', she replies, oozing sweet tones at me for the first time in our entire thirty-minute conversation. 'Not unless there's something else you want to know.' Heaven knows there are plenty of things I want to know, but she has already made it abundantly clear that these are things she doesn't want to tell me.

She asks me who I'm writing for, and I tell her it's a gay magazine called *Attitude*. There is a long pause before Donna Summer says, 'Just tell everybody I said "hello".'

So there you go, everybody – Donna Summer says 'hello'.

Bigmouth Strikes Again

Interview with Sandra Bernhard; November 1994

SANDRA Bernhard and I are relaxing aboard a flight from New York to London. We are sitting in the first-class compartment, flicking through our free newspapers, sipping our complimentary champagne, enjoying that extra bit of leg room.

Sandra insists on travelling first class these days. And why shouldn't she? After all, she has reached that point in the career of a modern icon where people she has never met before have developed an irritating habit of just walking up and introducing themselves. What's even worse is when people pretend not to recognize her – on a bad day, that can really bum Sandra out. So she travels first class, where nobody expects anybody to rush up waving an autograph book, and nobody is disappointed when nobody does. And besides, as Sandra so rightly says, how can a performer so committed to the idea of giving so much of herself on stage possibly deliver the goods unless she travels in comfort?

Sandra has asked me to refrain from smoking – she hates it when other people's smoke gets into her designer clothes. Today she is wearing a man's suit by Dolce & Gabbana. It's the kind of suit that women with her type of figure look especially good in. It is also a very comfortable suit, which is just as well since it's getting dark outside, and Sandra is feeling tired. When Sandra gets tired, her vulnerability shows through in ways you wouldn't expect.

'Oh Paul', she murmurs suddenly, turning to me with those big brown eyes of hers. 'Do you really think they'll like me in London?'

'Of course they'll like you, Sandra', I smile, reassuringly.

No I don't. And the simple reason for this is that, actually, not a word of what I've said is true. I made it up – not because I'm a complete fraud or anything, but because I was stuck for a way to describe exactly what it is that Sandra does. I don't mean how she defines what she does – you probably know that already. No, what I'm getting at is what Sandra Bernhard actually does – that strange talent she demonstrates through whatever medium she happens to be working in, that peculiar ability she has for blurring the boundaries between fact and fiction, and never quite losing the plot in the process. To put it bluntly, Sandra makes up self-aggrandizing, highly entertaining stories – little lies that tell the truth – about the captivating, corrupting influence of fame, about the strange scary nature of human sexuality, about the pain of growing up an ugly duckling in a world full of swans.

These stories dominate her work: the time Stevie Nicks drank two or three bottles of wine and practically begged Sandra to be her best friend; the time Sandra tripped on Ecstasy with a suicidally depressed Warren Beatty; the time she had to slap Madonna hard across the face because the poor woman was becoming so hysterical . . .

But let's get back to reality. Sandra Bernhard and I are sitting in her hotel room, and the atmosphere isn't exactly congenial. On the contrary, having already scared off the photographer, Ms Bernhard is now putting me firmly in my place. 'We're the creators', she says, meaning performers generally and herself very much in particular. 'We're the ones who are putting our asses on the line. You guys are just the ciphers. A few of you get it, and most of you don't. Most of you sit on your high horses with great pomposity and indignance, offering your critiques of people who just open their veins and bleed. Something has to be done about it, 'cos it's bullshit.'

She says this without any clear sense of irony, which in itself is ironic for a number of reasons. It's ironic because right at this moment in time it feels as though I am the one with their ass on the line. ('But surely you accept that critics have a role to play?' I protest, feebly. 'There's a role for intelligent critics', she snaps, still scowling. 'There's no role for stupid critics.') It's ironic because, as she was explaining to me only a few minutes earlier, 'There is not an ounce of cynicism or sarcasm in my work. It's all irony and great compassion. You can't create the kind of work I create and be a cynical person.'

But mostly it's ironic because, in spite of all her talk about blood-letting and agonizing creativity, Bernhard's one-woman stage shows are best appreciated as cool critiques of popular culture. Her latest, entitled *Excuses for Bad Behaviour, Part One*, is a departure from previous shows only in the sense that this time around she has an album and a single to plug. Otherwise, the format remains the same. Bernhard the upfront bisexual diva will impress us with her takes on other people's songs. She will entertain us with her stories about other (usually famous) people's lives. She will even, as she later admits, 'give a few readings from magazines'.

Actress, singer, comedienne, occasional fashion model and author of two autobiographical books (neither of which details her once much-publicized, now strictly off-limits relationship with Madonna), Sandra Bernhard has approached fame on her own uncompromising terms. The cult of celebrity – its attractions and its pitfalls – provides both the context and the content to her high-powered performances, whether it be running riot as the deranged fan Masha in Martin Scorsese's 1982 film *King of Comedy* (her first big break) or staggering on stage in a drunken send-up of Judy Garland, as she did a few years ago for the opening of her last show, *Giving Till It Hurts*.

At the time I assumed she was being ironic about the idea that only divas bleed. Today I'm not so sure. But that's okay with Sandra. 'Ambiguity is kind of my trademark in a way', she smiles, evidently satisfied that I'm not quite as stupid as she first suspected. 'I love walking that fine line with a song that may seem kind of geeky and superficial, and taking it and bringing something out of it. It's like when you hear a song by Lionel Richie and you think, "Oh god, it's Lionel Richie!" But then you realize that that song may have accompanied a moment or an experience that was very potent in some way, and so it becomes strangely beautiful. You're hearing this song you know is really geeky, and part of you wants to laugh, but at the same time it's pulling at your heartstrings.'

She professes a similar degree of ambivalence towards her own celebrity. For the encore to her 1989 off-Broadway show, *Without You I'm Nothing* (now out on video) she came back on stage draped in an American flag, apologized profusely for all the terrible lies she had told, and promised to 'cut the fame shit out for just this moment'. And then she unsettled everybody by performing a striptease version of Prince's 'Little Red Corvette'.

Today, she wants it to be known that she would just as soon cut the fame shit out altogether. 'I've gotten over the idea of doing this to be successful, or to be famous, or to be rewarded', she says. 'When you're starting out, and you want to establish yourself, you tend to be much more demanding. You want people to know who you are, and what you do. Later on, it kind of balances out. You don't have the same needs. And what you have to remember is that there are a lot of machinations to this business that are intriguing but somewhat destructive.' Like what for instance? 'Like constantly being in need of attention. Like always wanting the media to write about you. Like always wanting to be on talk shows. Like always needing to be in front of the public, as opposed to just going off and being creative, and then coming back and showing everyone what you've achieved.'

If I'm at all unsettled by this, it's probably because everything about her suggests that Sandra Bernhard takes her own celebrity very seriously indeed. While I don't doubt her achievements, or her ability to send herself up on record (listen to 'Manic Superstar' on *Excuses for Bad Behaviour, Part One* if you require any proof of this), in person she comes across as extraordinarily defensive and oddly humourless. Having read somewhere that she isn't exactly pleased with her new film, *Dallas Doll*, I let it be known that I quite liked it in parts. 'Did you?', she replies, her famous lips curling into a sneer. 'That's nice. I'm really happy for you.' For someone who claims not to draw on sarcasm, she can ooze it in bucketloads.

Or maybe that's just my misconception. People have a lot of misconceptions about Bernhard – journalists especially. They say her work is all about sex (it isn't). They say she can't sing particularly well (she can). They say she isn't funny (she is). Ask her to identify the most common misconception people have of her, and she answers immediately. 'That I'm just going to eat them alive. That I'm this really tough, hard, impossible, dramatic, larger than life bitch. Which is certainly part of my persona, and something I've used on stage to grab people's attention. It's very powerful. And I think it's very important. Women should be able to project that part of themselves, without being labelled a bitch. Unfortunately, we seem to have come full circle in our views of women. If you're a woman today you're supposed to just lay back and play stupid. That's not who I am.'

She's certainly right about that. She probably has a point, too, when she says that her biggest critics tend to be those people who are sexually repressed in some way. 'Why else would they be so fucking fascinated with my sex life? Unless they want to fuck me up the ass or something. Which they're doing figuratively anyway, so they might as well do it literally.'

But even though we end our conversation more or less as friends, even though she calls me 'honey' and thanks me for my time, I still leave Sandra Bernhard's hotel room convinced that if she were ever to do a cover of 'Fame', it would be the song sung by Irene Cara, not the one written by David Bowie. In other words, not the one that goes on about fame being hollow or (god forbid) making a person hard to swallow – the one that says simply, 'Baby, remember my name'.

Neil Tennant, Honestly

Interview with Neil Tennant, August 1994

IN April 1984, the Pet Shop Boys released their first single on Bobby O's Bobcat Records label, and the soundtrack to life in the gay 1980s changed course and speed. The original version of 'West End Girls' was a club hit on the American West Coast, and a minor success in France and Belgium. Re-recorded just over a year later, with Stephen Hague at the control desk, by early 1986 it had made number one in Britain and eight other countries worldwide. The Pet Shop Boys had arrived.

Although their working relationship was short-lived, ending somewhat disagreeably in March 1985 with Bobby O relinquishing all contractual rights in return for a substantial royalty return on future record sales, linking up with the legendary New York producer was a determining moment in the careers of Neil Tennant and Chris Lowe. Largely responsible for the Hi-NRG successes of club acts like Divine and Man To Man, Bobby O helped to define the sound of early 1980s gay disco. Having fulfilled their dreams of being part of the Bobby O story, the Pet Shop Boys turned the sound around, slowed it down, speeded it up again, and made it into something new, without ever fully divorcing it from its generic roots.

They also did something unthinkable: they wedded the euphoric sound of gay disco to lyrics which sounded very serious. Before the Pet Shop Boys, disco records were noted for the vacuity of their lyrics. In many instances, the words provided little more than verbal echoes to the all-important beat. The Pet Shop Boys were keen on the beat, too, but they weren't prepared to surrender everything to it. Even now, it is hard to imagine Neil Tennant ever completely surrendering himself to a typical disco lyric like, 'Oooh, love to love you, baby'. For one thing, it's too passionate. The Pet Shop Boys may have made records that spoke about passion ('I don't like much really, do I?', Chris Lowe deadpanned on 'Paninaro'. 'But what I do like, I love passionately'), but they have never been especially good at expressing it through song.

And of course the other point to make about a lyric like 'Oooh, love to love you, baby', the other thing that makes it not very Pet Shop Boys, is that, frankly, it is just too obvious. 'Obvious' is not a word one would normally associate with Messrs Tennant and Lowe. In spite of Neil Tennant's famous assertion that their music was a marriage between Hi-NRG and 'traditional song-writing, where the lyrics are interesting and make some kind of personal statement', the 'statement' part has never been very explicit. The truly 'ironic' thing about the Pet Shop Boys is that they have somehow managed to spin a career around the fears, the frustrations and (just occasionally) the fun of being young(ish), gifted and gay without being drawn into discussions about that all-important, always absent 'g' word.

'Obviously, people are going to look at our songs and read things into them', Neil said once. Obviously, but he also maintained that he and Chris were 'completely misunderstood anyway'. Refusing to clarify the situation, he kept stressing that there was a difference between what he and his musical partner might do in private, and what they were prepared to say in public. 'We've never said anything about our sex lives to the newspapers or to magazines', he told the *NME* in 1986. 'And we don't intend to.'

And they haven't. Until today, that is. Today, Neil Tennant has Something To Tell Me. He knows it and, thanks to a tip-off from one of those homosexual conspirators we're always hearing so much about, I know it too. In fact, this whole interview has been arranged on the basis of it. Only nobody has actually spoken about it – not even his press officer, who suggested that he and I meet twenty minutes before Neil arrived, just to get a few things sorted. I was expecting some kind of prep talk, something along the lines of, 'Look, Neil has decided to do this interview after a lot of careful thought, so please respect his feelings and please, please be gentle with him.' Instead, we had a friendly chat about life and the media in general and nothing in particular. All very pleasant, I hasten to add, but absolutely no help whatsoever in determining how I ought to broach the subject.

So here we are then, Neil Tennant and I, forty-five minutes into our agreed two-hour session and still the sticky question of what he does in private hasn't come up. Instead, we've talked about a lot of other, more public things. Why the Pet Shop Boys decided to do a charity record, for instance. 'We didn't actually decide to do a charity record as such', Neil informed me, a little crisply. 'We just had the idea of doing *Absolutely Fabulous* because both Chris and I love the programme, and we decided to do it for Comic Relief as a way of dealing with it, really. That way, we knew we wouldn't have any trouble getting the samples cleared by the BBC.'

We've talked about the Pet Shop Boys' contribution to the Kylie Minogue comeback album. 'Oh yes, the legendary Kylie album. Well, we always had to work with Kylie, of course, because she's such a trademark: "Kylie"! She's made it, really. She's just one name. We were asked if we'd like to work with her last year, but we'd just finished our last album and couldn't really be bothered to do any more. Then we wrote this song, and I said to Chris, "Oh, we should give this one to Kylie." I thought it sounded like Stock–Aitken–Waterman Kylie, which is exactly what she's trying not to do, unfortunately. But we sent it to the record company anyway, and they liked it, and she liked it. They've made it very different to the way we wrote it. It doesn't really have the same tune in it, for instance, and they haven't put the chorus in, but I suppose that's very modern.'

Largely thanks to the fact that Kylie is such a modern girl, Neil and I have sailed close to the wind a few times. We've talked about Kylie's gay audience, for instance, and the difficulty of broadening one's appeal without alienating one's core audience. 'I think it must be quite difficult being Kylie', Neil remarked at one point, to which my natural response was: and is it difficult being Neil Tennant?

'In what sense?' was his guarded reply.

In the sense of being misunderstood.

'Sometimes, though I'm learning not to care about it. It is obviously a failure of ours, that we have given people the impression that what we do is some kind of elaborate joke.'

So having established that it is obviously a failure of mine not to have given Neil Tennant the opportunity to clear up any lingering doubts anyone might have about whether he is or is not gay, I go off into a very long, very elaborate question about his impression of how the Pet Shop Boys are seen by the gay press, my impression of how their first album, *Please*, seemed to share a lot of common ground with Bronski Beat's *Smalltown Boy*, and how he felt about Jimmy Somerville's much-publicized accusation that he and Chris Lowe were exploiting gay culture for career purposes, and not putting anything back.

Neil Tennant draws a deep breath. 'The thing is,' he says, rearranging himself on the sofa, 'we were kind of stitched up by the *NME* on that one. They did an interview with us, and then they went on and on about hamsters. They never actually asked us, "Are you gay?" And then Jimmy Somerville was quoted everywhere, slagging us off. I thought it was quite arrogant of him, actually. He obviously thought that he had a right to talk about us in that way, and that his views on the subject were more important than our own views. His view is that the entire point of being a pop star is to be a positive role model. I reject any notion of being a positive role model to anyone. I personally find that an arrogant way to think of oneself . . . '

He pauses for a moment, realizing perhaps that this line of argument is only likely to open old wounds. 'When Bronski Beat came along, I was still assistant editor at *Smash Hits*. I loved those first few records. I loved the fact that they were gay, and that they were so out about it. It was the whole point of what they were doing. Jimmy Somerville was, in effect, a politician using the medium of pop music to put his message across. The Pet Shop Boys came along to make fabulous records. We didn't come along to be politicians, or to be positive role models. Having said all that, we have supported the fight for gay rights.' He reminds me at this point that the Pet Shop Boys were the only pop group to play 'Before The Act' in the fight against Clause 28. I remind him that they also appeared at last year's Equality Show on behalf of the Stonewall Group.

'And what's more,' he goes on, 'I do think that we have contributed, through our music and also through our videos and the general way we've presented things, rather a lot to what you might call "gay culture". I could spend several pages disputing the notion of "gay culture", but for the sake of argument, I would just say that we have contributed a lot. And the simple reason for this is that I have written songs from my own point of view . . . '

He pauses again, and leans a little closer towards the tape recorder. 'What I'm actually saying is, well, y'know, I am gay, and I have written songs from that point of view. So, I mean, I'm being surprisingly honest with you here, but those are the facts of the matter.'

Visibly relieved at having finally got all that off his chest, Neil Tennant pours himself a glass of mineral water and takes his sweatshirt off. He is looking distinctly pink around the gills. Perhaps it's the heat in here. Perhaps it's the embarrassment of finally admitting that for all these years he has been singing nothing but the truth. 'Well', he says, in a voice which carries a distinct sense of 'moving swiftly on'. 'What's your next question?'

The question everybody always asks about the Pet Shop Boys is, are they serious? And what they usually mean by that is, can such obvious displays of camp irony ever be regarded as remotely sincere? 'Yes', is Neil Tennant's immediate response, though of course it isn't nearly as simple as that. 'A lot of people seem to think that I'm not committed to what I'm singing about', he says, mournfully. 'It's partly because of the way I sing, I suppose. It gives everything a kind of distance. This isn't true for me personally. Personally, I think my voice is full of expression. At least that's how I hear it. But I know other people hear it as this cool, detached voice, and so they assume it's meant to be ironic. But it's just the style of singing I like, and also it's all I can do. I can't sing like Jocelyn Brown. Someone asked me once why people like me and Bernard Summer sang in this way, why we didn't put more vocal acrobatics into it. I said, "Well, it's because we're not good enough. We can't, I'm afraid. I'd love to be able to, but I just can't." But also it's the limits to your ability that create your style, ultimately. In pop music, style tends to be determined by what you can't do. That's why limitations are so important, and why pop music presents such a problem to consummate musicians. They don't have a style, because they don't have limitations. And so they end up playing jazz.'

Neil Tennant's fervent defences of pop music are well documented. So too is his tendency to get a bit defensive at the suggestion that what he regards as a passionate expression of deep feeling might be construed by other people as an exercise in camp excess. 'I never really think of us as being camp, typically', he says. 'But I suppose the idea of the Pet Shop Boys recording with Liza Minelli is camp in itself. We do occasionally do very dramatic things, like the start to "Left To My Own Devices", which is quite camp I suppose. But I think people use the term "camp" in the wrong way a lot of the time. The Liza Minelli album is not arch. It's a totally sincere record. Camp is naive. True camp has a totally one hundred per cent belief in itself. The thing about somebody like Liza is that she is very naive as a performer. She's just like that. The intention is never to be camp. The intention is to make something beautiful and exciting, something that will have the effect of lifting you away from your surroundings.'

Neil Tennant was born and raised in Newcastle. Although he has been known to speak fondly about his northern roots ('Chris and I are very proud of our northernness', he told a journalist a couple of years ago), he has also rubbished the notion that a sense of where you come from carries any real sense of belonging. ('I've never really admired regionalism', he said in the same interview. 'I've never admired tribal loyalties.')

His parents brought him up a Catholic and, from the age of eleven, he attended school at St Cuthbert's Catholic Grammar. Years later, he summed up his feelings about his school years on a song entitled 'This Must Be The Place I Waited Years To Leave'. 'It wasn't the religion I hated so much, really', he says now. 'It was the petty discipline. And it was a very sporty school. I definitely hated that part of it. But it made me what I am, really. It made me think, "Well, you're all going to have boring middle-class lives and I'm going to be a superstar!" In a way, it made me realize what I definitely didn't want to be.'

His feelings about Catholicism, on the other hand, were never so clear cut. 'When I was a boy, I always wanted to be a priest. Being me of course, I wanted to be the pope. I thought, if you're going to go in for all of that, you may as well be at the top, you might as well be number one. My parents insisted that I go to school, and that if I still wanted to be a priest at the end of it, then that would be okay with them. And of course by the time I was eighteen I didn't want to be a priest any more. I stopped believing in all that when I was about sixteen. I think you do at that age. It's a contest between religion and sex. The church tells you that masturbation is wrong. And of course you can't not masturbate at that age, so you have to make a choice between that and religion. Religion invariably loses out.'

By the time he'd reached the sixth form, the wanking would-be superstar had lost interest in school and taken to hanging around town with a few sympathetically minded friends. It was around about this time that he first began fantasizing about running away to London. 'I used to go and watch the trains pulling out of Newcastle Central Station at eleven o'clock on a Saturday night, and I used to think about how I could just get on a train and be in London in four and a half hours. It all sounds fantastically romantic, I know. But I had a very escapist view of things at the time. In some senses I still do. I still run away quite a lot, really.'

He finally made it to the capital in 1972. He studied history at North London Polytechnic, and worked at the British Museum to pay his way during the holidays. 'I still remember going to the interview', he says, laughing. 'I had to climb up this spiral staircase, and I was wearing women's wedge shoes, with four inch heels. I could barely walk. I had my hair cut short and dyed bright red. I got the job anyway. For some reason they quite liked me. The British Museum is a very strange place. There's a lot goes on behind the book shelves there.'

Graduating with a 2:1, he immediately got a job as the London editor of Marvel Comics, where his first assignment was to interview Marc Bolan. 'After that I worked in book publishing for a few years, then I joined *Smash Hits*, and then it was the Pet Shop Boys. So I suppose you could say that I was never being boring.'

Neil Tennant has a habit of doing this, of working snatches of his song lyrics into the conversation. In the course of our interview he managed to quote, at considerable length, the words to at least half a dozen of his favourite songs. Perhaps this is a sign of a complete lack of assumption: he really didn't expect me to be familiar with them. Or perhaps, in spite of how he once insisted that he was anything but a clever pop strategist, he can't resist an opportunity to show the world just how clever he really is.

It was while we were still on the subject of his education that Neil Tennant said the most extraordinary thing. Remembering how he was once hauled up before the headmaster to account for his lack of attendance, he gazed off into the distance and said: 'He called me into his office one day and said to me, "Let's face it, Tennant, you're soft, aren't you? You don't like school discipline." I just said, "Yes father, no father." And I thought, "What do you mean by that?" Of course I knew exactly what he meant by that. I was a classic poof even then, I suppose.'

He pronounced this last sentence with such an air of casual indifference, I forgot for a moment that this was Neil Tennant I was talking to. Neil Tennant, who once told a prying journalist that how he defined himself sexually didn't matter, 'only the songs'. Neil Tennant, whose favourite way of dealing with the fact of his homosexuality in his songs has been to reduce it to nuance and connotation. Neil Tennant, who writes lyrics in which the romance of homosexual longing is weighed up against the shame of homo-sexual wrongdoing ('It's a, it's a, it's a, it's a sin!'). Neil Tennant, who having taken all these years to publicly come out and talk about what he does in private, confesses that he still isn't really sure whether he wants to be known publicly as 'a classic poof', whether indeed he wants to be known publicly as anything.

'I knew a lot of gay people when I was growing up in Newcastle', he tells me when I push for a bit of sexual history. 'It was the early 1970s, and it was all divinely decadent darling, y'know with David Bowie being all androgynous, and *Cabaret* and stuff. I went out with girls at that time, and I sort of didn't want to be gay in a way. I didn't really like what I saw of the gay way of life, and I certainly didn't want to be a part of it. Then in the 1980s I realized that I probably was gay. I mean, by then I knew what I was attracted to. But I didn't really have a proper affair with anyone until three or four years ago, really. For most of the 1980s I was, well, not exactly celibate, but not far from it.'

Even today, he says, he would hate anyone to suggest that his identity was determined by his sexuality. 'I've never wanted to be a part of this separate gay world. I know a lot of people will not appreciate hearing me say that. But when people talk about the gay community in London, for instance, what do they really mean by that? There is a community of interests, particularly around the health issue, but beyond that what is there, really? There's night-clubs, music, drugs, shopping, PAs by Bad Boys Inc. Well I'm sorry, but that really isn't how I define myself. I don't want to belong to some narrow group or ghetto. And I think, if they're really honest, a lot of gay people would say they felt like that as well.'

It suddenly strikes me, after all this talk about defining yourself by what you don't want to be, about running away, about wrestling with a sense of belonging, that this – the gay community – must be the place Neil Tennant waited years to arrive at, only to discover that he really wanted to leave after all, and then find, to his intense frustration, that he couldn't, that other people wouldn't allow him to. 'I've always maintained that there was something worthwhile about my decision to make my lyrics generally applicable', he protests at one point. Then he adds, almost as if he was thinking aloud, 'If I was arguing with me now, I'd probably say "That's a complete cop-out, Neil." '

That's a complete cop-out, Neil.

'Yes, I suppose it is', he says glumly. 'But it sort of comes across anyway, doesn't it?'

Like many people, I first came across the Pet Shop Boys in 1986. I was at Heaven, watching a boy in a tight white vest dancing to 'Opportunities'. He wasn't being ironic. And neither, at the time, were the Boys themselves. Their first album, *Please*, positively bleeds with a sense of sexual longing. 'Opportunities' is in there, of course, but personally I've always thought there was something vaguely sexual about that song anyway. In the video, Neil, dressed like a proper toff, hangs around a garage, trying to solicit a response from a very sullen Chris Lowe: 'I've got the brains, you've got the looks, let's make lots of money.' Basically, it's a song about pulling a fast one, and there has always been more than one way of interpreting that. And then there are the slow songs, the soulful songs, the songs to make you cry, the songs about dressing up, going out, looking for love and finding disappointment. 'That boy never cast a look in your direction', Neil laments on 'Later Tonight'. I think what he really meant to say was, 'That boy never cast a look in *my* direction.' But never mind. As he says, it sort of comes across anyway.

It comes across in later lyrics, too: 'I love you, you pay my rent', 'Your life's a mystery, mine's an open book', 'Left to my own devices, I probably would.' Regardless of whether they ever wanted it to be read that way or not, the Pet Shop Boys have effectively set the changing pace of gay urban life 'to a disco beat', whilst staying in tune with the shifting moods of the times. If *Please* was about wanting a lover and going out late, *Actually* was about waking up and going out shopping, and *Introspective* was about wanting a dog and feeling, well, introspective. By the time the 1980s ended with *Behaviour*, Tennant and Lowe were writing songs about staying in, giving up smoking (''cos it's fatal'), and coping with the pressures of monogamy.

And the pressures of loss. The Pet Shop Boys arrived at precisely that moment when AIDS began making headlines in Britain. A year later, Neil Tennant's closest friend confided that he had recently been diagnosed as having AIDS. They'd known each other since they were fifteen. 'It all came as rather a shock to me at the time', Neil recalls. 'In 1986, it was still very shocking to know someone who had AIDS.' He registered his feelings on a song from *Actually*, entitled 'It Couldn't Happen Here', and for the next three years made regular visits to St Mary's Hospital. When his friend died, in 1989, he wrote a song about going to the funeral. 'Your Funny Uncle' describes the tensions that arise when a gay man's family and friends meet for the first time in order to pay their last respects. It was the flipside to 'It's Alright', a cover of a Sterling Void song, the lyric to which insists that everything is going to be all right, for the simple reason that 'the music plays forever.'

Actually, this isn't nearly as flip as it first sounds. In 1987, on a track called 'Hit Music', Tennant had wondered aloud about the changing function of music in a world with AIDS. 'It's a song about what happens when you take the sex out of dance music', he explains. 'What does music become then? It becomes a sort of insulator, a form of protection, of comfort.' And lest anyone concluded that he was being far too glib about all of this, the repressed anxieties surfaced a year later on 'Domino Dancing', where he sang about dancing with danger, adding another number to the score and watching 'them all fall down'.

'This year alone, three people I know have died of AIDS', he informs me. 'It's a lot. It's why I get angry when people go on about how AIDS is some kind of "fashionable disease". I mean, I don't know three people who've died of cancer this year, or heart failure, or multiple sclerosis. It's at the back of your mind all the time. Actually, it's at the front of your mind all the time.'

Having survived almost a decade of minding their language and feeling gloomy, the Pet Shop Boys ended 1993 with what many people (me included), consider their most obviously gay – certainly their least obviously closeted – musical statement yet. Neil Tennant refutes my suggestion that *Very* marks a departure from previous albums, that it is, in effect, the Pet Shop Boys' 'coming out' album. 'What you have to remember', he says patiently, 'is that all of our albums contain songs written over a period of twelve years. 'To Speak Is A Sin', which is on this album, was actually written in 1983. There's a song on the last album, called 'Nervously', which I wrote in 1981, before I'd even met Chris Lowe. It's about two people – sorry, two boys, or two men or whatever – meeting for the first time. And some of the songs on *Please* are as gay as anything we've done since. So I don't think it's entirely true to say there has been a radical progression in those terms.'

Perhaps not, but the decision to record a particular song at a particular time must count for something – it is at that moment, after all, that what was once a private thought becomes a public expression. And whereas the discreet coding of previous albums might have allowed straight listeners to avoid the point and accuse others of 'reading things in', only a complete and utter moron could fail to follow the plot of *Very*. Anybody who listens to Neil Tennant singing about dancing to disco, taking all of his clothes off, finding liberation in love, dreaming of the queen, waking from an AIDS-soaked nightmare and finally deciding to go west, and then arrives at the conclusion that this is not an album about what it means to be gay in the 1990s is quite clearly 'reading things out'.

'People will always have their own views about lyrics anyway', Neil says, sounding a little bored with the subject. 'Obviously, we've taken a lot of ideas about being gay and presented them to a heterosexual audience. Whether that is a good thing or a bad thing I couldn't really say.'

I've had this great idea for a title for the next Pet Shop Boys album. I think they should call it *Honestly*. I think *Honestly* is a very Pet Shop Boys word. Like *Please, Actually, Behaviour* and *Very*, it is very serviceable in as much as it manages to convey a variety of meanings all at once. 'Honestly' as in 'sincerely'. 'Honestly!' as in 'I can't believe you just said that!' 'Honestly?' as in 'I don't believe you for a moment'. In fact, it could be the name for the album the Pet Shop Boys never quite got around to recording, but very nearly did.

I am about to suggest this to Neil Tennant when suddenly, he decides to introduce me to another word in the Pet Shop Boys' vocabulary. 'There's a song on the B side of *Go West* called "Shameless" ', he tells me as he polishes off the last of the Evian. 'The lyric goes, "We're shameless and we'll do anything for our fifteen minutes of fame, we have no integrity, we're ready to crawl, to obtain celebrity we'll do anything at all." The song is an anthem to shamelessness, "shameless" being one of my favourite words anyway. I think you have to be shameless to be in pop music. You have to have some element of shamelessness about you, otherwise you simply couldn't do it. You'd be too embarrassed. For me, being in the Pet Shop Boys has always been a struggle between total embarrassment and total shamelessness.'

Listening to the tape of our conversation a few days later, I begin to wonder what the point of this strange confession was. Perhaps it was a reference to the fact that Neil Tennant no longer feels any sense of embarrassment about who he is, that his decision to go public about his private affairs means he has reached that point where he no longer looks back on his life 'forever with a sense of shame'. Or perhaps I'm reading too much into this. Perhaps it was simply his way of reminding me that he wouldn't normally do this kind of thing.

Honestly.

Part three

Men

Gay Acting

THE moment I met Jon, I knew he wasn't as other boys. Everything about him screamed 'difference', from his taste in clothes to his uncommon ability to recite all the best lines from *The Complete Works of Oscar Wilde*. Everything about him told me that here was a member of the male sex I could relate to, without having to pretend to enjoy really masculine pursuits like football, fist-fights and setting fire to my own farts. Everything told me, in fact, that I'd finally met one of those boys my mother had always warned me about.

Only he wasn't. Gay, that is. Back in 1984, in the days when 'New Man' was barely a gleam in an ad man's eye, and 'Queer' was a word no self-respecting queer would have used to describe himself, Jon was cheerfully blurring the boundaries between gay and straight men – not gay, but 'stray', or 'Gay Acting'. Oblivious to the demands straight society makes of its menfolk, he was attractive, sensitive and excessively camp. I was smitten. We even snogged – once – but it didn't lead to anything. He was too young and heterosexually fixated to fall in love with another man, and I was homosexually mature enough to know.

I'm not about to tell you how to spot a Gay Acting man. That would be silly. Gay Acting men are as diverse as the gay men they take after. There are Gay Acting doctors, Gay Acting teachers, Gay Acting (pretty) policemen, even Gay Acting electricians. Still, like the majority of gay men who are unable (or unwilling) to pass themselves off convincingly as straight, Gay Acting men tend to be most visible in the fields of arts and media. My boyfriend's brother, Joe, is a Gay Acting director of children's television programmes. My cousin, Oliver, is a Gay Acting illustrator.

Gay Acting men differ from straight men in just about every respect, but it is enough to say that they don't feel the need to prove their masculinity constantly, and that they're not driven by a fundamental fear and/or loathing of femininity – their own, or anybody else's. The only notable difference between Gay Acting men and gay men is that Gay Acting men tend to be predominantly heterosexual. Which isn't quite the same as saying that they've completely ruled out the possibility of ever having sex with another man. While the Gay Acting men of the 1970s glam era only played at looking gay so that they could lure women into (1) a false sense of security, followed by (2) bed, the Gay Acting men of today take it as given that their heterosexuality is far from immutable – there is always the possibility that the right man simply hasn't presented himself yet.

For a man to be Gay Acting he must first be gay-friendly. And it seems only fair to ask that gay men return the compliment. However gratifying it may be to kid ourselves that there are some things only a card-carrying, 100 per cent bent, pinko, penis-obsessed gay person could possibly get their head around (hence the T-shirt slogan, 'It's A Gay Thing – You Wouldn't Understand'), the truth is rather different. Harvey Fierstein got it completely wrong when he argued that straight actors should be excluded from playing gay roles on the grounds that they were incapable of playing them convincingly. As somebody with a far queerer conscience than mine once observed, as gay men we're all in the business of making this up as we go along – learning to play the part convincingly is an intrinsic part of the game.

Gay Acting men exist to remind us that gay identity isn't something you're born with, like an unusually large penis or an abnormally small hypothalamus. It's something you have to apply yourself to, like a particularly obscure lesson in algebra, or a method for getting in and out of a rubber vest without dislocating an elbow. No man becomes gay through an accident of nature. It requires dedication, discipline and an ability to commit every episode of *Dynasty* to memory. Failing that, hard cash will do just nicely. These days all it really takes to persuade the world of your gayness is a fat wallet and a few shopping trips up Queer Street.

Gay Acting men came out of the closet in their thousands during the 1980s. If the 1970s were the best time for being gay, the 1980s were the decade for faking it. Partly this was brought on by the mass marketing of consumer pleasures previously branded 'effeminate' to men previously branded 'Neanderthal'. Partly it was prompted by the fact that the decade's chief movers and shakers – from George Michael to Boy George to the Pet Shop Boys – were either gay themselves or making a fair performance of it. Before them there was Bowie of course, and way before him there was Elvis. In fact it's probably true to say that the biggest names in the history of popular music have tended to be the Gay Pretenders. When Elvis wiggled his pelvis at the Grand Old Opry back in the mid 1950s, one observer took exception to the king's queeny application of eye-shadow, and was moved to comment that 'it was like seeing a couple of guys kissing in Key West'.

Only in one vital respect it wasn't. There is very little risk involved in coming across like a big girl's blouse when you've got a bunch of hulking great security guards strategically positioned between you and the swirling masses (Brett Anderson please take note). It takes balls of steel to strike out alone and boldly parade your difference where no Gay Acting man has gone before – Orping-ton for instance, or anywhere within a ten-mile radius of Swansea.

Which is why I think it is high time Gay Acting men were given a bit of credit, actually. It is one of society's most closely guarded secrets that the overwhelming majority of heterosexual men are no less obsessed with each other's private parts than homosexual men are; it is the public demonstration of gayness that gets the homophobe's goat. Gay Acting straight men are as vulner-able to anti-gay violence as Gay Acting gay men are, and far more likely to be queerbashed than any man (gay or straight) who is Straight Acting and good at it. One Gay Acting man of my ac-quaintance has been queerbashed more times than any gay man I know – and on more than one occasion he had a girl on his arm.

So the next time you're down your local gay bar and some petty-minded queen starts whinging on about how he can't stand heterosexual men, ask him to explain exactly which heterosexual

95: *Gay Acting*

men he is referring to. And if all he can come up with is that tired old line about how all heterosexual men are basically the same and basically share the same prejudices when you get right down to it, knee him sharply in the groin and then offer to piss in his lager. It's a straight thing – he wouldn't understand.

Masculinity: Complex?

IN the beginning there were Real Men, then came the Village People. Part parody, part fetish, part defensive self-representation, the hyper-masculinity of late 1970s gay urban culture had a profound impact on the culture at large. It doesn't take a degree in social science to work out why. If masculinity could be reduced to a handful of readily attainable signifiers (faded Levi's, checked shirt, handlebar moustache), how was a regular guy supposed to tell the genuine Joes from the queer imposters? The gay appropriation of macho styling marked the beginnings of one almighty case of homosexual panic. When gay men started hopping aboard the flight from the feminine, it was high time for the straight boys to bail out.

And they did, in their thousands. The year 1978 was not a good one for Real Men. It wasn't merely that the pleasures of hanging out with all the boys at the Y had been given a queer slant on *Top of the Pops*. It wasn't simply that Sly and Arnie weren't especially big that year. 1978 was also the year the ground-breaking magazine *Achilles Heel* was launched. Its agenda? To provide a forum in which men could explore new ideas about masculinity in response to the dilemmas posed by feminism. In other words, a magazine for men which didn't pander to the solid-gold, easy-action formula. It was enough to drive a construction worker to reconstruction classes.

But not enough to keep him there. For all its pioneering zeal, *Achilles Heel* was steeped in an already obsolete socialist rhetoric. If, as Jonathan Rutherford has suggested (*Men's Silences*; Routledge, 1992), the guilt-free consumerism of the early to mid-1980s provided a new language for changing masculinities (by relaxing men's anal-retentive refusal to take pleasure in the looks of other males), it did so at the expense of radically changing men. (I think George Michael probably summed it up best when he said 'Wham, bam, I am a man!')

Just as feminism and the politics of gay liberation had provided fertile ground for the gestation of what we now refer to as 'Men's Studies', so they continued to produce its star pupils. As late as 1987, R. W. Cornell observed that 'Most of the radical theorizing of gender has been done by women or gay men.'

Since then we've seen the fall of New Man, the rise of Iron John, the birth of the Backlash, and too many books by angry young and not-so-young men intent on proving those bloody feminists wrong, but only proving them right with their heedless misogyny. If you're left in any doubt that modern masculinity is in a serious state of crisis, just check out the publishers' catalogues. The first wave of Men's Studies gave us touchy-feely titles like *How Men Feel* and *Men Freeing Men*. The recent wave is awash with defensiveness and fury: *Refusing to Be a Man, No More Sex War, Not Guilty.*

Masculinity is a slippery concept – even more so when it's wet and whiney. Nine out of ten academic commentators seem to agree that the main problem is the need to engender men properly before engaging them in the debate. Ask your average man what 'Gender Studies' is, and he'll tell you it's got something to do with women wanting to burn their bras and cultivate their body-hair. While most men spend the greater part of their lives thinking about penises (usually their own, though often someone else's), they rarely think of themselves as possessing a gender at all. As Peter Middleton observes in *The Inward Gaze* (Routledge, 1992), 'Men have written plenty about themselves as men; little of it consciously.'

The problem with the bulk of what passes itself off as 'Men's Studies' is that it too takes masculinity as a given. But what makes a man a man? Masculine identities and responses can be, indeed usually are, mediated through other identities – class, race, sexual orientation – yet the experiences of white, middle-class, heterosexual men are still accepted as the structuring norm. Ironically (or perhaps not so ironically), it has taken a woman to challenge properly the assumed universality of this single male subject and try out 'alternative ways of inhabiting a morphologically masculine body'. In *Male Subjectivity at the Margins* (Routledge, 1992), Kaja Silverman examines a variety of masculine identities which fall outside the phallic pale and occupy a psychic space traditionally defined as 'feminine', before concluding, somewhat plaintively, 'after even a partial glimpse of those pleasures and psychic possibilities, who would still opt for the straight and narrow path of conventional masculinity?'

The unfortunate truth is, quite a lot of men actually. As anyone who has ever tuned in to Radio Four's *Locker Roor* programme can testify, patriarchy fucks up both men and women, but it fucks up women a whole lot more. (I think that oh-so-radical bisexual butterfly Ziggy Stardust probably summed it up best when he said 'Wham, bam, thank you mam!') Producing the right noises on the airwaves is all well and good. At the end of the day, the boys are still calling the tune; we shouldn't really be surprised when, in spite of their fondness for words like 'sensitivity', 'mutuality' and 'clitoris', their actions make it clear that they'd rather it be one they can dance to.

And that's assuming they want to try a different tune in the first place. Even as Men's Studies begins to show signs of getting into the groove of modern feminist and queer thinking, the so-called Men's Movement is leading men up the garden path and into the woods to reassert an unqualified masculinity – a masculinity defined solely by its negation of femininity and paranoid fear of homosexuality. Rather like the men's cosmetics boom, all this noise about changing masculinity may turn out to be little more than a face-saving exercise.

Stepford Boyz

LISTEN, I have Something To Tell You. I have spent a lot of time mulling over the consequences of this. I have racked my brains for the right words, the best way, the safest way to broach the subject. Because, what you may or may not realize is, I'm taking a major risk by telling you this at all. For all I know, you might react badly. For all I now, you might be One Of Them. But I have to tell someone, so it might as well be someone as physically removed from me as you are at this moment in time.

The thing is, I'm not 'Gay'. What I'm really trying to say is, I'm not entirely happy about what it means to be 'Gay'. And before some earnest agony uncle recommends that I rush out and buy myself a copy of *How to Be a Happy Homosexual*, let me just point out that I've read it, it didn't speak to me, and in any case it isn't the sexual aspect of my homo-identity that I'm unhappy about. I don't mind being homosexual one bit. It's this thing called 'Gay' that's driving me crazy.

GAY – three little letters that mean so many things. Pardon my language, but whose bright idea was it that the political awakening of 'homosexuals' should depend on a word the spelling of which was shorthand for the phrase 'Good As You'? Whoever it was, I'll bet he's choking on his words now. It may be a phrase we're still going through, but what was once a powerful declaration of self-worth (i.e., homos are every bit as good as heteros) is now little more than an excuse for every consumer queen from here to Old Compton Street in London's Soho to feel really good about himself and his empty-headed hedonism.

See them wherever there is a pose to be struck and a few pink pounds to be squandered (on cappuccino, mostly, though some do stretch to itsy-bitsy lyrca one-pieces). Watch them as they go about their daily routine of primping, preening and perking their tits up at the gym. Study them closely, and you'll be forced to agree that our booming 'Gay' scene has spawned a generation of Stepford Boys – sorry, 'Boyz'.

There. I've said it. If you haven't already reached for the phone, then I'm probably in the clear. You're probably not one of them. But you're bound to know who I mean. 'Boyz.' Now there's a sign of the 'Gay' times if ever there was one. You have only to flick through a copy of Britain's most popular 'Gay' freesheet to see just how far we've come. You only have to digest a few pages to understand that, these days, it is not only possible to pursue a life of 'Gay' pleasure without sparing a thought for gay politics – it's what's expected. 'What's the point of concentrating on the down side of being gay (whatever that is) instead of gorgeous pop, handsome boyz and good times?' opined Simon Gage, editor of *Boyz*, in a typically fun-packed issue. Well Simon, perhaps it has something to do with the fact that in the big, bad world beyond Boyztown, those experiences commonly referred to as 'the down side of being gay' (that's institutionalized homophobia, queerbashing, AIDS, little things like that) continue to impact rather heavily on people's lives.

Of course it's no surprise to anyone to hear that boyz just wanna have fun. When all's said and read, their favourite publication is simply a reflection of their favoured existence. And what an existence it is. While the sterile world of the Stepford Wife makes her swear she'll die if she doesn't get that recipe, the puerile world of the Stepford Boy makes him swear he'll stay in if he can't do like the song says and give himself over to absolute pleasure.

And there's no reason why he can't. Because, like the row upon row of supermarket aisles which provide the Stepford Wife with the daily sedative she needs, everything in the Stepford Boy's world is ordered to ensure that he derives the optimum amount of consumer pleasure from his every waking moment – provided, of course, that he is willing and able to pay for it. He wants sex? Here's a cruise bar, a wank mag, an 0898 number. He wants to go shopping? Here's a male order catalogue, a shop full of 'Gay' goodies, a street full of 'Gay' shoppers. He wants to get completely off his face and dance till dawn with his arms wrapped around a beautiful stranger and a bottle of poppers jammed up one nostril? Here's a club. And another. And another. I'll say one thing for the Stepford Boy: he certainly knows how to party.

I know what you're thinking. You're thinking that all this sounds suspiciously like so much 'Queer' talk. Well, I guess that pretty much depends on what your definition of 'Queer' is. I used to think that 'Queer', with its promise to boldly go where no movement had gone before, would find better places to hang being 'out' around than the 'Gay' emporium. Now I realise that, for most queers at any rate, 'Queer' is simply 'Gay' with knobs and nipple-rings on. Queer campaigners are doing a commendable job combating homophobia. But where are the queers prepared to challenge the Boyz Own Vision of what a 'Gay' identity could, or should, be?

'Gay Is Good' was the slogan we used to sing, back in the days before we all went shopping. Well, I'm sorry, but no, actually, it isn't – at least not always. Not when it is used to bankroll mediocrity. Not when it means paying over the odds for second-rate goods and sloppy service, simply in the interests of making a few rich 'Gay' men very rich indeed (and then have them add insult to injury by telling us they're only in it 'for the good of the community' – a bit like saying Marks & Spencer are working for the good of all single people living in Britain, simply because they stock ready meals for one).

In the penultimate scene from Bryan Forbes's 1974 cult film *The Stepford Wives*, our heroine, Joanna (played by Katharine Ross), comes face to face with the woman she is destined to become. Backing into a room that looks remarkably like her own bedroom, she discovers an exact replica of herself (a clone, if you prefer). In the logic of the film, only one of them can survive. So Joanna dies, and her doppelgänger finally gets her hands on that recipe everyone has been talking about.

The tragedy of the Stepford Boy is that the boy he once was lives on inside of him. And there will come a day when he will suddenly decide that he never wants to see that recipe again. He will wake up under his rainbow sheets, stagger into the bathroom and be forced to face the fact that, one day, even Stepford Boyz are obliged to become men. And as he looks at his dark eyes in the mirror, he will feel hopelessly alone. Because in Boyztown, as in Stepford, no one can hear you scream.

Demolition Men

A FUNNY thing happened on the way to the 1990s. A sub-species of *homo sapiens* with bulging biceps, bad accents and no self-irony suddenly developed a sense of humour about all things mean, mumbling and muscular.

I am referring, of course, to the Hollywood Action Pack. Personally, I have always thought there was something faintly ridiculous about Sly, Arnie and the rest of the brute boys. When a man is so hung up about his height that he wears stacked shoes (as Stallone is rumoured to do), or so conscious of his weight that he pumps iron to the point where he passes out (as Schwarzenegger frequently did back in the pre-*Terminator* days), you're hardly inspired to look on him as a potential role model. When said man then runs around with a bazooka over his shoulder and no shirt on his back, begging you to measure his masculinity by the calibre of his hardware and the size of his tits, the only conclusion you can possibly draw is that he is a bit, well, *hysterical*.

Funny as it might sound, for the best part of a decade and a half it has been practically impossible to grope your way around the local Odeon without being bombarded with invitations to take such extreme examples of macho posturing seriously. From Stallone's violent exploits in the three *Rambo* films to the breezy pyrotechnics of Schwarzenegger's *Terminator* and *Total Recall* years, the 1980s were a decade in which masculinity asserted itself through brutal demonstrations of musculature in motion. Possibly as a response to a perceived depreciation in traditional male expressions of power, the Hollywood action films of the period highlighted the pumped-up male body as a self-serving (and self-preserving) source of spectacle – a trend best exemplified by the solitary figure of John Rambo, stripped off and ready to take on the world.

Inevitably, this baring of the male body opened up the possibilities for a fair amount of homoeroticism. More importantly, the emphasis on external (physical) capabilities over internal (emotional) resources effectively distracted the audience from the question of conscience. The action hero was simply 'a man' (or, in Arnie's case, a man-machine), driven by circumstance to perform acts beyond the average man's capabilities – not least of which being the recuperation of the masculine ideal as a legitimate object of envy. While a film like *Rambo*, with its combination of proletarian struggle and gung-ho jingoism, seemed to feed off quite complex Reaganite fantasies of US nationalism, and a film like *The Terminator* played on compound fears of what a post-nuclear future might hold, the unifying message of the 1980s action films was actually very simple: fuck feminism, it's still a man's, man's world.

Nowadays, straight men have a rather different perception of themselves. In the caring, sharing 1990s, a man can still get away with just being plain nasty, but it's so much nicer to be thought of as nasty but knowing. This is the reason why a magazine like *Loaded*, which goes out of its way to celebrate all the worst aspects of straight male behaviour, chooses to address its target readership as 'men who ought to know better' – the implication being that of course they do know better, but larking about with the lads is such a bloody good laugh, and when all is said and done, there's no real harm in it, is there?

The desire to be nasty but knowing, and have a laugh into the bargain, is also the reason why spoof action films like *Loaded Weapon* enjoy a level of success way beyond the quality of the gags involved. The mere fact that Schwarzenegger made a film called *The Last Action Hero* suggests that the Hollywood money men know the days of the 'straight' action man are numbered. Producers are finally recognizing that we live in an age where the values embodied in displays of extreme physical masculinity are becoming increasingly difficult to maintain, or at least a hell of a lot harder to package and sell. The solution? Wrap it up in irony. Make 'em laugh, and the chances are they'll be fooled into believing you were never being serious in the first place. It's a bit like when you're caught out telling a whopping great lie – the best option is to pretend that you were only joking all along.

The first member of the Action Pack to see the market potential of this strategy was Schwarzenegger. A large part of Arnie's huge success comes down to the fact that he has always been one giant step ahead of the crowd. Way back in the early 1980s, when Stallone was still playing for sympathy as the winning underdog with puppy eyes, Arnie was happily firing harpoons through people before cheerfully telling them to 'stick around'. But with later

Schwarzenegger vehicles, the joke often ran far deeper, drawing attention to the various constructions on which his entire 'acting' career is based. There is a scene in 1989's *Total Recall* where Arnie's character is asked to step back and consider his position: is he really an intergalactic spy caught up in a conspiracy, or just an ordinary manual labourer plagued by paranoid delusions? As Yvonne Tasker has pointed out in a recent essay on action movies, 'Dumb Movies for Dumb People', 'the moment is funny . . . because as a star and as a character within the film Schwarzenegger inhabits both positions – an extraordinary, ordinary guy caught up in a nightmare narrative' (in *Screening the Male: Exploring Masculinities in Hollywood Cinema*, ed. Steve Cohan and Ina Rae Hark (Routledge, 1993, p. 241).

In many respects, *Demolition Man* represents Sylvester Stallone's stab at *Total Recall*. For starters, it's a big-budget, futuristic fantasy (complete with references to virtual reality), which derives many of its 'ironic' touches from the audience's assumed familiarity with its star. But far more importantly, *Demolition Man* acknowledges the existence of other action heroes too (including Schwarzenegger), and then sets out to prove that Stallone, while older and in some respects less well-equipped than his competitors, can still beat them to the bad guy. This is one star vehicle that lets you know exactly where it is heading. *Demolition Man* isn't just another action film on which another ageing action hero is pinning his hopes of salvaging a career; it's a film which explicitly illustrates its star's frustrated ambitions. Having dismissed Rambo as 'a pussy' in *Tango and Cash*, Stallone now attempts to cash in on the joke.

The Demolition Man of the title is John Spartan (Stallone), a tough-talking, hard-acting cop from the year 1996 who is frozen alive for breaking the rule book, then thawed out some thirty years later when the authorities of the day prove ineffectual in tracking down a particularly nasty villain. Spartan's old-style brute tactics are perceived as a godsend in a world where the 'tyranny' of political correctness has prevented the police from enforcing order (they've swapped their guns for assertiveness training), and one-time action heroes like Schwarzenegger have been reduced to lending their names to town libraries.

The girl in the story (in a Stallone film, she is always a 'girl') is a pretty policewoman who dreams of life in the uncomplicated 1980s, has a *Lethal Weapon* poster on her wall and has been secretly waiting for a good old unreconstructed guy like Sly to come along and help her get to grips with all these silly anxieties she has about exchanging bodily fluids. Because we are supposed to think of her as a bit of a feminist, it is she who makes the first pass, inviting him to engage in a bit of virtual reality, ultra-safe sex. Sly, naturally, is having none of it. A quick round of tonsil tennis is all it takes to erase the memory of AIDS, plus two similar (fictional) epidemics from her mind. Perhaps this is what people mean when they say Italians do it better.

Barely effective as a straightforward action thriller, deeply reactionary in spite of its 'ironic' touches, *Demolition Man* is a flashy catalogue of sadistic pleasures for the intellectually impaired. It says a lot about the anxieties at play within Hollywood (and within the straight male audience for which this film is presumably intended) that what could have been an entertaining satire on macho values is simply a self-reflexive little parable about the future of good old-fashioned action heroes in a world where the future, if not entirely female, is increasingly feminist.

Rather like Kyle Reese, the time-traveller who pitted his wits against Arnie's sheer physical force in *The Terminator*, Stallone has travelled through time in order to rescue the future. But the only future Stallone is interested in saving is the future of the particular version of masculinity he is capable of performing. And if his performance here is anything to go by, it is hardly one worth preserving.

Singing Lessons

COMEDIAN Harry Enfield calls them 'ponces'. But you don't need to be straight and stupid to miss the point of opera queens – gay and stupid will do just fine. We've all seen the small ads in the gay press: 'No fats. No fems. No Maria Callas fans'. In his book *Queens* (Quartet, 1984), gay author Pickles dismisses the gay patrons of the opera house as 'supercilious', 'snobbish', 'piss-elegant' and 'unstable'. Often stereotyped as over-emotional, snivelling individuals given to extreme flights of fancy and a fragile grasp of what makes a man a man, opera queens fill the slim-fitting shoes of all those sad young men who stood in for homosexuality back in the days before the first macho clone was 'liberated' into a good, solid pair of workman's boots.

Is it any wonder so many gay men seem as keen as their straight counterparts to put the boot in? In these post-liberation days where queer masculinity is measured by queer 'musculinity', the opera queen gives the game away for what it is – a game. The body gay men go for nowadays is taut, smooth, hard; the opera queen's body is characteristically limp, flabby, soft. In a world where gay men are taught that our bodies are something to be ashamed of, something to be controlled, regulated, conditioned into shape, the opera queen's body is always making the 'wrong' statements, always signifying extremity, always expressing 'excessive' emotions. And as many a good opera queen knows to his cost (dinner for two and a wadful of notes to some escort agency), the vast majority of gay men prefer the strong, silent type.

In his remarkable book *The Queen's Throat: Opera, Homosexuality and the Mystery of Desire* (GMP, 1993), Wayne Koestenbaum charts his obsession with opera and the divas who gave good throat. 'The opera queen', wrote Pickles, 'is usually a frustrated diva longing to wear a big glittering frock and powdered wig.' Turning this pickled thinking on its head, Koestenbaum argues that the diva is actually an embodiment of what it means to be homosexual. 'Divas talk like Oscar Wilde', he observes, before adding, almost by way of an afterthought, 'Or Oscar Wilde talked like a diva.'

Which came first – the diva or the queen? Like popular images of gay men, divas are often perceived as perverse, abnormal, deviant. ('I adore the unusual', confessed Jessye Norman.) A diva creates herself. Her gestures are rehearsed, her appearances staged. (Remember the first time you went to a gay bar, how you took note of the way the other men dressed, danced, moved or simply stood about in what Neil Bartlett once described as 'that casual yet significant manner'?) A diva is said to 'come out' from behind a curtain at the start of a performance. (Annie Lennox, who would like to be thought of as a diva, though never as a lesbian, describes 'coming out to perform'.) In performance, a diva's voice 'comes out' from her body in a way that can often sound 'unnatural'. (J. K. Huysmans wrote in a letter that 'sodomy changes the voice'.) Like queers, divas have often taken the blame for natural disasters, moral corruption, even the destruction of empires. (When Mrs Elizabeth Billington debuted in Naples, Vesuvius erupted. In the 1936 film *San Francisco*, a modern-day Sodom crumbles at the sound of Jeanette MacDonald's operatic tones.)

The first opera Koestenbaum ever saw was *Aida*. By the last act he was, he recalls, 'exhausted'. Years later, he caught his first *Madam Butterfly*, and was shocked to discover that, like men, opera frequently kills the thing it loves. I have never seen *Aida*; I have a bad recording of *Madam Butterfly* on tape; I have been to the opera on no more than three, possibly four, occasions. Still I think I know a thing or two about diva worship. I mean, I was present the night Barbra Streisand performed at Wembley; I did once have an affair with someone to the tune of Shirley Bassey singing 'The Rhythm Divine'; I do own more than one biography of Judy Garland (my friend Gordon says he always thought the circumstances of Garland's life were something a gay man picked up by osmosis the first time he performed a blowjob).

A lot of nonsense has been written about gay men and their divas. In a book entitled *Opera, or The Undoing Of Women*, Catherine Clément urged Maria Callas's gay fans to 'leave this woman alone, whose job it was to wear gracefully your repressed homosexual fantasies'. There is still a persistant homophobic belief that gay men distort popular art forms to suit their twisted psyche. The most common charge is that gay men's obsession with divas is inherently misogynistic, that we derive sadistic satisfaction from watching them turn and burn. Either that, or our strong identification with divas is a symptom of our innate self-hatred, our 'internalized homophobia'.

The point the critics usually miss is that it isn't the diva's self-destructive urges gay men most identify with. Now more than ever, it is her fight for survival. In *A Star Is Born*, Judy Garland's character explains how she somehow feels most alive when she is asked to perform. At a time when silence does, literally, equal death, there is a lot riding on the simple assertion, 'I Could Go On Singing'.

Drug Queens

THE truly remarkable thing about recreational drugs – the thing that makes them such an essential part of modern gay male identity – is that the mere act of popping, snorting or shooting them can turn even the most uptight, middle-class queen into a sexual outlaw.

This isn't my opinion. It's the opinion expressed by one of the men interviewed in a Channel 4 *Out* item on gay men and drug use broadcast on 16 August 1994. And judging by the fact that what he says goes unchallenged, that nobody responds by saying, 'Actually, that's a load of pretentious twaddle', you can't help but suspect that it is probably the opinion of the programme-makers, too.

The programme in question is called *Drugs R Us*, but don't be misled. Far from treating gay men's relationship with drugs as childish, writer Chris Woods and director Tony Gregory set out to prove that there is a lot more to Ecstasy, cocaine, etc., than their uses as toys for the boys. And give or take the odd overstatement ('You just can't be a card-carrying homo today unless you take drugs', someone suggests at one point), they do succeed in making us think carefully about the origins and dynamics of contemporary club drug culture.

Still it has to be said that the most revealing comment in the entire twenty-four-minute programme comes when one anonymous E head explains that he'd rather sit at home alone than go clubbing without drugs because 'I can't fit in if I'm not off my head'. Drug use has always been as much about fitting in as it has been about dropping out. I have a friend who, each time he takes Ecstasy, announces to anyone within earshot that the music is inside him. All he is really saying is that he has lost his inhibitions, that he feels completely at one with the world – or at least with the thousand or so other clubbers all grinning madly and moving to the same beat. Escapism, coupled with a desire to be in with the in crowd, plays a far greater part in determining most people's decision to take a trip than some juvenile fantasy of turning into William Burroughs.

I'm not saying that gay men nowadays don't have good reason to take drugs. God knows, we all deal with enough crap in our daily lives to make our demands for bigger, instant pleasures now look like the small rewards they really are. I just happen to think that there is a world of difference between getting high in order to escape the pain of life that you, I and our friend Madonna apparently know only too well, and kidding ourselves that our little acts of escapism amount to something resembling a revolution.

There are times when even I am inclined to take drugs seriously. Approach me at around 1 a.m. on a Saturday night, and I'll happily inform you that the arrival of Ecstasy was the most profound moment in the history of the gay scene – ever. All I'm really suggesting is that we would all be better advised to keep that type of talk for the dance floor, where the only people listening are likely to be other E heads similarly predisposed to interpreting chunks of meaningless drivel as a series of mindblowing revelations.

Because it doesn't matter how many books on sex magick you've read, it doesn't matter how much you can read into the bleeping noises on the latest Belgian techno import – drugs do not make you a more interesting person. On the contrary, they have a nasty habit of making most people considerably less interesting than they were to start off with. And far less attractive. Take too many Es at the weekend, and by Wednesday you'll have a complexion like dried-up pizza. For a gay man, that's a pretty serious consideration. I mean, why spend half your salary on skin products, only to squander the rest on substances clinically proven to rob your skin of all those precious liposomes?

And I haven't begun to mention the various ways in which drugs wreak havoc with your mental and emotional stability. You may be high on a happy vibe for a few hours, but there's a strong chance you'll be a sad fuck by sunrise. And for some time afterwards. Anyone who has tripped the Saturday night light fantastic with the help of what is laughingly referred to as a 'designer drug' will know all about that messy Monday morning feeling. Choose a dodgy designer, and Monday can last right through till Thursday – assuming, of course, that you live to see Monday in the first place. Let's not mince words here: drugs can really screw you up.

To give Woods and Gregory fair credit, *Drugs R Us* does outline many of the negative side-effects of regular drug use. One user describes a particularly bad acid trip. A drugs counsellor reminds us all that 'there is no such thing as a free buzz', and explains how prolonged use of any powerful stimulant will invariably lead to paranoid psychosis. But the pop promo style of the programme – all bright lights and trippy camera angles – distracts attention from the gravity of what is being said. And because the overwhelming majority of the men interviewed chose not to appear in front of the camera, there is no sobering visual counterpoint to the tantalizing glimpses of washboard stomachs and pumped-up, sweaty pectorals.

Unless of course you count the brave appearance by gay publisher and self-confessed 'speed-freak' Peter Burton. Remember, kids – drugs may do all kinds of weird and wonderful things to your mind and body, but they won't always make you slim.

Brawn in the USA

IF Bob and Rod Jackson-Paris were ever asked to pick a song for *Our Tune*, the song they'd probably choose would be 'Muscles'. Recorded by a woman with little grasp of irony (Diana Ross), written by a man with an even weaker hold on reality (Michael Jackson), this whimpering tribute to the over-developed male form sums up everything you need to know about America's first gay couple.

In the land of free weights and expensive dentistry, Bob 'n' Rod cut quite a profile. Their joint autobiography, *Straight from the Heart*, was a gay bestseller. They've been photographed by Herb Ritts, and interviewed by Oprah and Donahue. Hardly surprising, really, since their story is the stuff of which talk shows are made. An ex 'Mr Universe' and a former *Playgirl* centrefold, Bob Paris and Rod Jackson meet (at the gym, naturally), fall head over heels, and get hitched in one of those gay marriage ceremonies some people are going in for.

Then the real labour of love begins. Turning their backs on the worlds of women's porn mags and knobbly knockers contests, they sweat their way through a series of books, photo-shoots, videos and television appearances, gradually building up a reputation as shining examples of all that a gay life can be – happy, wholesome and bursting with love and pride. Not to mention bland, vacuous and shamelessly narcissistic.

And very few people do – mention it, that is. In a culture where pecs are widely regarded as a prerequisite to sex, the gay body politic has taken Bob 'n' Rod to its heart. Posterboys for what Andrew Sullivan, gay editor of the *New Republic*, has called 'the second wave' of gay liberation (i.e., queers who just wanna be like everyone else), the Jackson-Parises are treated with a level of respect normally reserved for right-wing lady politicians with dubious track-records and impressive hairdos.

The American gay lifestyle magazine *Genre*, in an attempt to justify its claim that they were the right men for 'the Herculean task' of teaching the world that 'gay is okay', did its best to identify some brains behind the brawn. What seemed to matter most, though, was that Bob 'n' Rod were 'handsome, masculine and conservative'.

According to *Genre*, 'when Bob and Rod make an appearance, several million homophobes are disarmed. Such influence can change all our lives'. *The Advocate* took a rather more critical view, asking whether mimicry of the straight institution of marriage was damaging to the gay movement.

The irony is that Bob 'n' Rod, for all their masculine good looks and conservative assimilationist energies, couldn't successfully mimic straights if their membership of the local health club depended on it. The problem isn't that they are 'straight acting' – it's that they are so awfully 'gay'. Need convincing? Then I suggest you take a look at their most recent book. A visual portrait of a gay marriage, *Bob & Rod* claims to break 'totally new ground in the annals of photogaphy'. This is one way of alerting you to its contents, which consists mostly of butt-naked shots of our two heroes as they go about the daily business of being gay, married and proud.

The opening section, entitled 'Pools', features Bob, Rod, a few fig leaves, a snake, and lots of cool blue water. Then it's off to the Rocky Mountains for a spot of nude wrestling, followed by a quick cuddle at the cabin, a few hours larking about on the houseboat and a journey through 'Various Edens' (beaches and woodlands, mostly), before returning home to the pet poodle and parrot. Some day, all gay lives will be made this way.

In his fawning introduction, photographer Tom Bianchi expresses his sincere gratitude to his subjects, and sincere wish that his book might stand as a testament to 'the naturalness and goodness of the love expressed here'. Fat chance. Maybe it's my natural aversion to seeing men with short legs and too many muscles making such spectacles of themselves, but a photograph of two grown men larking about in the snow with only their love and matching pairs of Timberlands for comfort does little to warm the cockles of my big gay heart.

On the contrary, I start to wonder whether any self-respecting straight wedded couple would subject themselves to this degree of public humiliation, just to prove a point (though a similar portrait of Richard and Cindy's marriage might have been good for a laugh). And it doesn't matter how many poses our two heroes strike, it doesn't matter how many rocky landscapes they're shot against – nothing can disguise the fact that, basically, what we're dealing with here is a pair of Muscle Marys with no sense of proportion.

Which would be fine, if that was all they were cracked up to be. Only, of course it isn't. Having swapped the competition stage for the lecture podium, Bob 'n' Rod have made a career out of promoting themselves as role models, and on that score they're not looking too good. Contrary to changing hearts and minds by challenging 'negative' stereotypes of gay men ('Look, Mabel, bodybuilders can be queer too!'), they reinforce the most enduring and damaging myth of all – that while heterosexuals have real lives and real emotions, we fags have only lifestyles and an unlimited capacity for self-love.

Still they are enormously popular. Which draws me to the worrying conclusion that perhaps Michael and Diana aren't quite as out of touch as I first suspected. When it comes to the question of role models, maybe they were speaking for all of us. Maybe all we really want is some strong man to hold on to.

Soap Dish

WHEN I was barely twelve years old, Elsie Tanner touched me. Pat Phoenix, the actress who breathed life into *Coronation Street*'s scarlet woman, came to my home town to open an 'up-market' amusement arcade called Stardust. For some reason I never could quite work out at the time, I'd always had a bit of a soft spot for Elsie. And so it was that one small-town boy with stardust in his eyes, and about fifty large women with shopping trolleys, stood in the rain for over an hour.

When she finally arrived, stepping out of a big black car in a leopard-print fur coat and sunglasses (sunglasses! in a town where the sun never shone!), we all surged forward, eager to catch a glimpse of the woman who made the drab world of Weatherfield seem as electrifying as London's West End. And it was at that point that Elsie Tanner touched me. On the upper left arm. Just below the shoulder. On the very same spot where I now have a tattoo – of a phoenix.

Some things you never get over, and I have never lost my love for *Coronation Street*. I think in one sense my sympathy for a fallen woman like Elsie prepared me for being gay. Not that I ever felt the slightest urge to leap on the first man bearing more than a passing resemblance to Len Fairclough (Elsie's taste in men always left a lot to be desired). But she was a survivor in a situation where the greatest sin was to survive, a square peg in a hell-hole of a place where the net curtains were always twitching with disapproval. The Enas and Annies of the world could say what they liked: Elsie Tanner was what she was.

I was recently asked by a straight journalist from a straight newspaper whether I thought *Coronation Street* could be 'justified' as gay cult viewing when, unlike some other soaps, it had never done us the service of featuring a gay character. I sometimes have to laugh at the importance heterosexuals place on being earnest. They are so used to seeing themselves represented everywhere, they tend to forget that for some of us at least, seeing isn't always believing. *Brookside* and *EastEnders* may have had their gay Gordons and their kissing Colins, but *Coronation Street* has always been the queen among soaps.

'Is it because the women look like men in drag?' this journalist wanted to know. Not exactly, though on reflection I'd say the reverse is often the case. The first rule of a good soap is that the women must be strong, and it is certainly true that the female residents of Weatherfield generally possess a larger-than-life quality which tells us they were cut out for far more than a boring coupling in a back street could possibly offer.

The real drag acts, however, are the men. They may not have big hair and bigger ear-rings, but the men who live on *Coronation Street* clearly know a thing or two about the comic potential of gender performance. In most cases, they exaggerate (or subvert) the characteristics of their gender to such a degree that they become laughable. And, almost to a man, they make such a performance of their heterosexuality, you really can't help but suspect there's something a bit funny going on. In *Coronation Street*, straight courtship is such a constant source of amusement, we are rarely inclined to take the romantic clinches seriously.

Ten reasons why *Coronation Street* is queer television: Reg Holdsworth's water-bed; Jack Duckworth's pigeons; Steve MacDonald's eyebrows; Mike Baldwin's packet of cigars; Kevin Webster's packet; Curly Watts's love-life; Des Barnes's brother; Percy Sugden's moustache; Don Brenan's perm; Mavis Wilton's Derek.

There are other factors to consider, of course. Back in the 1970s, Bet Gilroy (then Lynch) had a poster of David Bowie poised as Ziggy Stardust above her bed. I used to wonder whether they ever met up to exchange fashion tips. When someone bought me *The Coronation Street Cookbook* for Christmas a few years ago, I was shocked to discover that no one had thought to include what my boyfriend refers to as 'The Bet Lynch Breakfast': two fags and a pot of tea. Popular culture, it is often said, feeds on itself: without Debbie Harry there would never have been a Madonna. Queer culture is often the uninvited guest at the table: without Bet Lynch there would never have been a Lily Savage.

Things can sometimes go awry when an invitation is extended the other way. When Elizabeth Dawn (alias Vera Duckworth) played to a rowdy gay audience at The Fridge in London, the set resembled Jack and Vera's living room, the 'act' amounted to a portrait of a marriage in which the cracks are always showing.

Inevitably, Dawn lost the crowd's sympathies when she tried to smarten the performance up with a song and a posh frock. It was like hearing Rita Fairclough speak in a proper voice, the equivalent of impressionist Mike Yardwood announcing 'And this is me'. Reality has never much been a part of *Coronation Street*'s charm.

The fabrication of realism, on the other hand, has. On my bookshelf I have a book called *Weatherfield Life*. In it you can read up on the prehistory of *Coronation Street*, on the turbulent lives and loves of the characters who resided there before the cameras started rolling in 1960. What it all adds up to is an alibi, an excuse for suspending disbelief in what patently didn't happen. And just to ensure that we don't take the lie too seriously, anything remotely resembling authenticity is shattered when we reach the final pages, enter the here and now, hear Curly Watts tell us he's 'petrified' by his 'magnetic sexuality'.

Failed seriousness is the essence of camp. The people who make and market *Coronation Street* know that. Bill Hill, who edits *The Street*, the soap's bi-monthly magazine, thinks the programme is increasingly aware of its gay audience. 'With those over-the-top performers I would say they are pushing the programme towards that market', he recently told *The Independent on Sunday*. 'We have a big gay readership in the magazine.'

If you need further proof of *Coronation Street*'s innate queerness, check out the merchandizing. For years you've been able to buy T-shirts emblazoned with the faces of favourite *Coronation Street* characters: Bet, Vera, Hilda Ogden. Nowadays they come with slogans that play on the discrepancy between how the characters see themselves and how they are seen by us. The best-selling T-shirt in HMV, Oxford Street, during summer 1993 featured barmaid Raquel Wolstenhulme and the slogan 'Je M'Appelle Raquel – Je Suis Une Supermodel'.

My own personal favourite features a grinning Reg Holdsworth and the slogan 'A Man Of Natural Appetites'. Reg, bless him, is about as 'natural' as the world he inhabits. Which, as every sensible adult knows, makes for the best kind of fairy tale.

Hetero Hell

TWO things you already know about straight men: they are dangerous when drunk, and they can't dance to disco. Now something you possibly didn't know: the vast majority of straight men are totally immune to the effects of Ecstasy. Honestly. The love drug has no effect on them whatsoever. Give your average straight man a tab of E and he'll be about as lovey-dovey as if he'd just downed five pints of lager and caught you stealing a look at his pint/arse/girlfriend. And no, he still won't be able to dance.

I made this alarming discovery one lost weekend when, by an unfortunate twist of fate, I found myself at a south London club, the name of which I am sworn never to repeat in print (here's a clue, though: it sounds a lot like 'misery'). Having survived a close encounter with Godzilla the doorman (No, I'm not an international terrorist, now kindly loosen your grip on my pancreas), I make my way up a metallic ramp, and present my ticket at the first checkpoint.

By the time the third checkpoint looms into view, and the third stern face inspects my crumbling piece of paper, I am coming to the conclusion that this is no ordinary night out on the town. Forget the bright lights, the blaring music and the terminal queues for the loos. Forget the customary, earth-bound, run-of-the-mill adventure in clubland. I am preparing myself for the flight of my life.

'Fright' would have been more appropriate. Who was it who decided that only homosexuals could possibly find their way around the twilight zone? Whoever it was, they obviously forgot to inform this lot. The women, by and large, are fabulous – all lipstick, lycra and shiny, happy faces. They're out for a good time, and they're smart enough to know that, straight men being what they are, good times come in small packages – usually with a little bird or a big fat heart stamped on one side.

But the men? The men wouldn't know a good time if it walked up and offered them a few fashion tips. And heaven knows most of them could do with a few. Didn't the age of the brave New Man teach these people anything? Most of them wouldn't look out of place on a football terrace. Only then they might at least look as though they were enjoying themselves.

I can't understand it. Ecstasy is the drug that puts you high on a happy vibe, right? I know. I've seen it working. Drop in at any big gay club and you'll find plenty of gay men who've dropped an E or two (or three, or four). They are the ones pulling funny faces at the lighting rig, oblivious to the fact that the regular DJ has buggered off on holiday and left his dear old mum in charge of the decks. Most of them are waiting for something to happen – Mr Right to walk through the smoke and sweep them off the feet, or Mr Right Now to offer them a quick blowjob in the loos. In the meantime, they're content to carry on partying – smiling as they dance, dancing as they smile.

Not this lot, though. I know they're on E because they've all got mad staring eyes and bottles of tap water tucked into their back pockets. So how come they look as though their favourite team just lost a home match? They skulk around the dance floor in their saggy jeans and puffa jackets, sullenly shifting their weight from one foot to the other, grimly focusing on the person in front – the breasts, if the person in question is female; the feet, if it's a fellow male. And woe betide any man who breaks the rules and invades their personal space. 'What's your problem, mate?' one particularly sad specimen snarls as I inadvertently brush past on my way to the loos. No problem at all, mate, save this sudden, overwhelming desire to smash your miserable face in. (Sometimes, even gay men can't help acting on impulse.)

That wouldn't be a very wise move, though. A quick survey of the crowd suggests that myself and my three companions are the only queers here. There's a couple of guys in tall hats and tiny T-shirts wiggling away at the edge of the dance floor – but that doesn't mean they're gay, that just means they're desperately uncool.

Standing at the urinal, doing my best to mind my own business, I am accosted by a tall, red-haired man with eyes on stalks, wanting to know where he can get some 'whizz'. I tell him I don't know, and his face settles into a very unpleasant stare – like it's my fault I don't have drugs coming out of my armpits. Butch as I am, this guy is quite clearly a loon. I smile weakly, turn away and concentrate on the job in hand.

When I turn back, old bug eyes has gone – to harass some other poor punter I don't doubt. I walk over to the wash basin.

Reflected in the mirror, I see a group of lads hovering around one of the cubicles. Bug eyes is amongst them. Something tells me it isn't a quick blowjob he's after. I don't know what the man they're all waiting for is giving them, but I know I don't want any of it. I decide it's high time I left the twilight zone to its natural inhabitants and went somewhere more exciting – like home.

Buns of Steel

IS it a bird? No. Is it a plane? No. Is it a new breed of superhero, come to carry us up, up and away from all the hetero-sexist bullshit that swamps the Saturday evening TV schedules? Er, not exactly. It's the man from the 'Frosties' ad, the one Tony the Tiger coached in the art of volleyball. And he's wearing tights.

Superman flew back on to our television screens in February 1995, and I can't think how I ever got through a Saturday night without him. Dean Cain cuts a far finer figure in that silly blue suit than Christopher Reeve ever did. He's got the perfect gym-honed body. He's got the dazzling Colgate smile. He's got the regulation gayboy bunny Calvin Klein briefs keeping his super bits in order. And so far as I can tell, he's got buns of steel holding up the rear.

Is it really any wonder that gay men are going gaga? 'Cain is more than Super', gushed one overexcited contributor to the Amer-ican gay 'zine *Spunk*. 'He's fabulous! He is the Clark of my dreams. A Superman who seems like he'd be just as comfortable in West Hollywood as in Metropolis. A Superman for all of us!' Personally, I'd prefer the phoneyness of Metropolis to the phoneyness of West Hollywood any day of the week, but we get the picture.

The view is actually a little different from across the pond. The programme may be a huge hit with the boys who fly the rainbow flag, but the American TV networks are less upfront about our hero's queer appeal than John Birt's 'glad to be grey' BBC. In the States, *The New Adventures of Superman* goes out under the title of *Lois and Clark* – the implication being that the relationship between the go-grabbing Miss Lane and the inexplicably modest Mr Kent is the show's main attraction.

I can't see it, myself. As every dedicated Super-fan will surely agree, the primary motive for keeping up with his latest adventures isn't to see how many romantic clinches Clark and Lois get them-selves into – it's to see how many times the camera can catch Dean Cain in his underwear. Evidently, somebody on the production team feels it necessary to remind us that Clark's modesty doesn't stretch to his own living room. And while the baring of his flesh may make stimulating viewing for gay men and straight women alike, the playful way he conceals his true identity, coupled with the outrageous campiness of the scripts, makes the new Superman a peculiarly 1990s, peculiarly queer spectacle.

Of course there was always something a bit suspicious about the man of steel – all that hanging around in telephone boxes and underwear worn as outer-wear. All the new model really does is make the queer elements more explicit. But how much more explicit. Right from the very first episode, when wise old Momma Kent advised young Clark that, dressed in *those* tight red trunks, he needn't be concerned about people checking out his *face*, the programme makers have seen to it that Clark's secret life is viewed in terms which draw attention to the sexual side of his nature. And if counting the number of crotch shots in each subsequent episode makes it seem as though I'm putting all my queer eggs in one well-hung basket, well, there are other places to point to for evidence.

The second series got off to a flying start with poor old Lois getting a taste of what it means to live a double life. To cut a long story short, the late Lex Luther's ex-wife cloned her in an attempt to tarnish her golden girl reputation. Cloning is clearly a popular pastime in Metropolis. In the first series, Luther managed to clone Superman himself. Naturally (or perhaps not so naturally), the clone wasn't nearly as well-adjusted as the original, and so spent most of his time larking about in his boxer shorts, demanding piggyback rides from his 'daddy'. When the two men of steel met, hovering face to face high above the city, the clone came over all coy and bolted. His parting words, if my memory serves me correctly, were: 'Catch me if you can!'

Of course none of this provides conclusive proof that Superman is actually gay. For that, we'd really need to catch him in the act, or else find someone else who had. Judging by past episodes, I'd say Jimmy Olsen was the best bet. Certainly he seems to have developed quite a crush on Clark, as evidenced by his habit of calling him 'C. K'. Yet in all the times that Superman has flown off with Olsen in his arms, he has never once attempted to shove his tongue down the cute cub reporter's throat.

Still it would appear that the new man of steel has one X-ray eye on his gay audience. 'I've always been concerned about Superman', one fine, upstanding resident of Metropolis complained during the cloning of Lois episode. 'Why is he so secretive? What has he got to hide?'

What indeed? Here's looking at you, C. K. I won't tell if you don't.

Confessions of a
Tattooed Loverboy

'IS this going to hurt?', I asked in the faltering tones of someone who just knows the answer is going to be 'yes'. 'Not if you relax', he said gruffly, laying out his equipment and slipping his right hand into a disposable latex glove. The radio was playing 'Something's Gotten Hold Of My Heart'. Mine was oscillating somewhere between my oesophagus and my mouth. Feeling a firm grip on my trembling flesh, I focused on a dent in the table-top and thought of a few of my favourite things . . .

What more can I say? He lied. (Add *that* to the list that starts with 'Your cheque's in the post' and ends with 'I won't come in your mouth'!) Getting my first tattoo (what the hell else did you think I was talking about?) was a painful operation. The solid black outline was bad enough, but when it came to putting in the colour and shading, I felt like James Dean competing for the title of human ashtray. And it didn't end there, either. Then came the sleepless nights, the itch you couldn't scratch, the scab you picked when you shouldn't have, the tube of Savlon all squeezed out. Only after three interminable weeks could I finally bare my insignia to the world, and a pretty insignificant one it turned out to be, too.

That was over three years ago. Since then, I've put myself through the same ordeal a further four times. What started out as a discreet sacred heart, commonly mistaken for a strawberry, has gradually evolved into a complicated skulls-and-daggers affair that stretches halfway down my arm. When I finally ran out of right bicep, I turned my attention to what was on the left. This time I went for it in a big way, and paid good money to a man who put me through two hours' worth of pain in one sitting. Either I'm finally learning to relax (an unlikely proposition, as anyone who knows me well enough can verify), or I've fallen prey to the kinds of masochistic urges that simply aren't satisfied by what I do in bed.

What is it about gay men and tattoos? A glance through the small ads section in any gay paper is all it takes to determine that the ancient art of tattooing holds an aura of sexual fascination for the modern gay man. One free paper even has a specially compiled section for tattoo enthusiasts. When I came out, in 1984, every man I met wanted to go to bed with a flat top. In 1984, I was sporting a wedge and making the best of enforced celibacy through mind-expanding reading. By 1985, I had a flat top and had been well and truly introduced to the benefits of socially expanding cloning. Tattooed loverboys are the new flat tops, the clones of the 1990s. Their image appears on club flyers, on T-shirts, on the covers of gay magazines, in the latest pornography from Europe and the United States. Lately, I've been struggling to understand why. Having already joined them, I'm desperate to beat some sense out of them – not literally, you understand, but in the sense of just wanting to make sense.

I started by delving into my own psyche. I've been entertaining fantasies about Genet – all those prisoners huddled together in the dark, penetrating one another with dark glances and pinpricks. I've given no end of thought to the bad boys of my youth – swaggering out of the local tattoo parlour, proudly displaying their blue smudges, boasting that it didn't hurt a bit. I've even tried putting the blame on Tim Curry – what was that homo-sexually loaded question 'Do you have any tattoos, Brad?' if not a rallying call to a whole generation of would-be Rockys? The naughtier the suggestion, the better it sounded. Like many a gay man whose only act of teenage rebellion was joining the local drama society, I glowed in the knowledge that my tattooed flesh would cause far greater alarm to my parents than the fact of whom I shared my bed with. (My mother probably knew I was gay long before I did, but when it came to sitting down and talking about my tattoo, well, I was *the last person she'd have thought it of.*) So what if I never skipped school, never got a girl pregnant, never got caught smoking behind the bike sheds, never did drugs? It's the quiet ones you've got to watch out for, after all. Having a tattoo was supposed to open doors to the ranks of the outsiders – the prisoners, the bad boys, the no-good punk scum who haunted the erotic subconscious of my overly literate, sickeningly wholesome college-boy persona . . .

Sounds dead sexy, doesn't it? Only that isn't the way it turned out. I've been forced to face the truth, and it's not half as ugly as I'd hoped. Deviation, depravity, sex had nothing to do with it. Genet's sadistic, scatalogical prison fantasies couldn't be further from the picture, and I couldn't hold down a bad boy if I tried. I'm a queen, and such are queens that, as with many other things, getting a tattoo all stems back to my obsession with Oscar Wilde. 'One must be a work of art, or wear a work of art', the least sexy of all my idols wrote a hundred years ago. I've taken his directive at face value. I figured that was the only way to take it.

The point of this confession is to illustrate the fact that you can't talk about tattoos without talking about myths. The greatest myth, the one that drives more people into getting tattooed than any other, is that tattoos represent something deep and meaningful. The truth, as Oscar would have pointed out had he lived long enough to witness our latest fixation, is that all tattoo art is surface and symbol. An effective tattoo (one that appears to say something about the wearer) is only ever a variation on an established set of culturally encoded themes – love, hate, sex, religion, death. I've overheard aficionados insisting that having a tattoo etched into their too, too temporal flesh produces an altered state, a kind of primal consciousness. In a postmodern world of transitory passions, a tattoo is a token towards immutability, but that's all it ever is – a token. The 'modern primitives' interviewed in the controversial *Re/Search* classic (1990) describe the experience of being tattooed as 'a passage to another life'. Forget it. 'Images have become our true sex object, the object of our desire', observed Jean Baudrillard in a moment of rare lucidity. Exhibitionism, machismo, fetishism – these are the impulses that put most people under the needle, not some urge towards antediluvian anarchy.

Which isn't quite the same as saying that having a tattoo isn't, at some level, a form of revolt. In Western society at any rate, tattooing still carries a distinct anti-authority appeal, the origins of which are to be found in the early Christians' condemnation of the practice, and the subsequent moves towards prohibition across Europe. (An indication of just how differently things developed in the East can be seen in the Anatomy Museum at the University of Medical Science in Tokyo, where over a hundred tattoo skins are lovingly preserved.) For centuries the exclusive preserve of criminals and degenerate aristocrats, Western tattooing boomed in the 1890s with the invention of the first electronic tattooing machine, the evolution of which has kept pace with the demands of each successive generation of would-be reprobates, from drunken sailors to bombed Millwall supporters. The punks made a not-so-fine point of having every conceivable part of their anatomies tattooed, and look what a revolting lot they were. With punk came the philosophy of fashion as corporal rebellion – if you can't afford ownership of anything else, you can at least declare ownership of your own body. And if walking into the job centre with a spider's web etched across half your face hardly improves your chances of employment, well that's just the price you have to pay for being in the club.

It's this expression of tribalism, coupled with (and to some extent compounded by) the urge to transgress social restriction, that is part and parcel of the naive, if colourful, attraction of tattooing in the Glad To Be Grey 1990s. Like a safety-pin through your nose, or a sneaking diabolic passion for herb tea, a tattoo is only as transgressive as the company you keep. I recently had an argument about adornment with a friend who'd just returned from a visit to the tattoo parlour. We were propping up the bar at one of Soho's trendier gay watering holes. Tattoos, he proclaimed, were an anti-fashion statement, a token of one's point-blank refusal to be party to the capitalist conspiracy known as the fashion industry; these transitory comforts weren't worth the psychological hunger they fed off.

I watched him take a swig from his bottle of Mexican beer, studied the wedge of lime as it slid down the inside of the glass, stirring up a froth in the appropriately chilled liquid. His grip on the bottle as he raised it to his lips made his bicep bulge, causing his tattoo to swell and at least five pairs of hungry eyes to turn admiringly in our direction. I opened my mouth to speak, thought better of it, and rolled up the sleeves of my T-shirt another half inch. Surround yourself with tattooed loverboys and you can have a very colourful sex life. Just don't kid yourself you're part of anybody's revolution.

Part four

Cinema

What Are You Looking At?

LONG before Madonna posed the question with her 'Vogue' single and video, the black and Latino queens of Harlem were striking a variety of poses which, intentionally or not, question the way we think about identity. Their lives (or rather, the versions of their lives they were willing to offer to camera) are the subject of Jennie Livingston's award-winning documentary, *Paris Is Burning*. The title of the film is borrowed from Harlem's largest annual drag ball – one of a series of events at which local queens compete for attention and trophies by dressing up and parading their fantasies of femininity, high fashion and affluence.

At first glance, the competitions seem like little more than alternative beauty contests. Competitors doll themselves up, bitch at each other, and strut up and down a makeshift catwalk, all under the watchful eyes of the judges. The ultimate accolade is to be proclaimed a 'legend' – a word which, of itself, draws attention to the dynamics of the game. To be described as a 'legend' is certainly to be talked about, but it is also to have doubts raised about one's true origins. The discrepancy between origins and ambitions is one of the main tensions present in the film. Shot in and around the ball scene during the years 1987 to 1989, *Paris Is Burning* focuses on a group of disenfranchised individuals (poor, gay, black), whose dreams of escaping 'the pain of life' they know only too well are acted out through imitations of the kinds of people (rich, straight, usually white) they aspire to be.

If their desires fail the test of political correctness, it's probably because some people can't afford the luxury of policing their fantasies. If, for Madonna, 'life's a ball', for these wannabes the ball *is* life, or at least the only part of it worth making a song and dance about. In the terms we usually employ to measure quality of life in the material world, these queens have plenty of nothing: many come from dysfunctional families, a large number are homeless, most are living hand to mouth. In the terms of the culture they have created for themselves, they can have, and be, just about anything they want – at least for the duration of the evening. 'OPULENCE!', someone screams out at one point. 'You own everything! Everything is yours!' And as if the irony of such claims wasn't obvious enough, another competitor spells it out: 'the voguing balls are our fantasies of being a superstar'.

Or a Wall Street executive. Or a military man. Or a mannequin. Or even just part of the family. Family is of paramount importance to these dreamers, and it isn't terribly difficult to work out why. In the life organized around going to the ball, each contestant is a member of a 'house', which is really just another name for a gay street gang. Each house has a family name ('Labeija', 'Ninja', 'Pendavis', 'Xtravaganza'), and at the head of each there is a 'mother' and a 'father'. The remaining members are known as 'the children'. Each competes for the glory of his (or 'her') house.

To describe the occupants of these houses as a 'pretended family' is not to insult them. The expression is actually a very useful one – not because these gay family units are in any sense less meaningful or less secure than the model sanctioned by straight society (indeed, in these children's experience, the opposite tends to be the case), but because the very phrase 'pretended family' draws attention to the terms under which all gay identities and relationships are routinely examined and found wanting. What *Paris Is Burning* asks us to consider is whether such terms are really ever that useful in the first place, whether anything is ever simply 'real' or 'pretended'. As the children take to the floor in borrowed (or, more often, stolen) robes, and the judges award points to those who achieve 'realness' (i.e., pass as someone or something other than their 'true' self), it isn't Madonna's instruction to 'strike a pose' that comes into play but Aretha Franklin's gutsy challenge, 'Who's zoomin' who?'

To underline the point, Livingston juxtaposes footage of the competitors vying for prizes in the 'realness' stakes with shots of 'real life' rich girls going about their daily shop, showing us that, when all is said and done, the art of appropriation is a hall (or mall?) of mirrors. It's a reminder of Judith Butler's observation that gay isn't to straight as copy is to original, but as copy is to copy. In this context, the phrase 'What are you looking at?' isn't simply an expression of attitude. It is also a serious question: what, exactly, are we looking at? A gay man acting the part of a 'real' woman? Or a gay man acting the part of a person referred to as 'woman', who is in turn acting the part of a 'real' woman?

Not that everyone featured in the film is attuned to such ironies. When one drag queen explains her desire to be 'a real woman' by arguing that 'real women have an easy life', it's clear that there is a fair amount of good old-fashioned fetishism lurking behind the banner of queer parody. But to dismiss these people as simply 'pathetic' (as a reviewer in *The Times* did when *Paris Is Burning* occupied BBC2's *Arena* slot in 1990) is to miss the point of the exercise. What Livingston has set out to show us is how, in the dizzy world inhabited by the ball queens, the 'realness' of identity itself is repeatedly called into question. If their tendency to equate possession of certain consumer goods with possession of a whole new identity strikes us as absurd, on reflection it is no more absurd than a yuppy couple signalling their social position with a few shopping trips to Habitat, or a butch queen putting on a leather jacket and convincing himself that it makes him more of a man. If the ball queens' purchase on commodity fetishism appears to take consumerism to its logical extreme, it alerts us also to the extent to which all identities are, in a sense, purchased.

It is these burning questions of identity that make *Paris Is Burning* such a 'difficult' film, and such an important one. In a review of the film published in *The New Statesman* (9 August 1991), Quentin Crisp complained that the organized subculture depicted in the film was part of 'a process of re-ghettoisation', and one which is 'gay-inflicted'. On the contrary, *Paris Is Burning* shows us a subculture articulating its uneasy relationship with the wider, straight world. If the story beyond the film is one in which reality bites – in which drag queens live in fear of the violence inflicted on them by queerbashers and pop stars make a mint out of their temporary investments in a culture they have no proper understanding of – perhaps this serves only to make the desire to escape all the more comprehensible. And if the people getting away from it all on the dance floor seem at times hopelessly dazzled by the stars in their eyes, it's probably worth remembering what the gay-coded, straight-identified George Michael once said (and I'm only too happy to paraphrase): 'It isn't that something extra that makes someone a superstar, it's that something missing.'

Killing Time

'The one duty we owe to history is to rewrite it.'
• *Oscar Wilde*

HISTORY repeats itself. Historians repeat each other. Gay men go to the movies. Usually for a bit of good old-fashioned escapism. Sometimes to complete the gaps in our history. Just occasionally to protest at the way our lives have been represented.

In 1980, in New York, gay activists picketed the opening of William Friedkin's leather-queen psycho-thriller *Cruising*, handing out leaflets claiming, 'Gay People Will Die Because Of This Film'. In 1992, Queer Nation took Hollywood to task over its 'negative stereotyping' of lesbians and gay men as psycho-killers in films such as *JFK*, *Silence of the Lambs* and *Basic Instinct*. When *Basic Instinct* opened in San Francisco, the activists were there, waving placards that declared, 'Films Like This Encourage Hate, Violence and Discrimination Against People Like Me'.

Death, hatred, violence, discrimination. In his book *The Celluloid Closet*, the late Vito Russo assumed a direct causal relationship between the representation of homosexuality in *Cruising* and the fact that 'in November, 1980, outside the Ramrod Bar, the site of the filming of *Cruising*, a minister's son emerged from a car with an Israeli submachine gun and killed two gay men'. Russo didn't say whether the killer had actually seen *Cruising* or not, but the idea was clearly planted: 'A Gay Person Did Die Because Of This Film'.

There is no conclusive proof that films perpetuate violence, but it suits some people to say so. In our 'free' society, films are censored on the basis of what some people think they know, and what they think they know still depends to a large extent on their interpretation of conflicting evidence. One thing we know for certain is that fears of film influencing social behaviour are often used as arguments against the funding and distribution of lesbian and gay work. That gay activists should be promoting the idea that 'negative' representations lead to 'negative' actions therefore raises a few rather awkward questions about queer political strategy and the homophobic uses of censorship.

And of course what few people stop to ask themselves in the heat of the protest is this: if by 'People Like Me' we mean 'People Who Have Sex With People Of The Same Sex', then what, exactly, are 'People Like Me' really like?

Historical fact: in 1923, in Chicago, two Jewish law students kidnapped and killed a fourteen-year-old boy named Bobby Franks. Apprehended in a matter of days, they were brought to trial and sentenced, each receiving ninety-nine years plus life. They showed no remorse for their crime, nor any real motive. They did it simply to confirm their sense of intelletual superiority, and to demonstrate their emotional commitment to one another. Nathan Freudenthal Leopold Jnr and Richard A. Loeb were child-murderers with the looks of matinée idols. They were also lovers.

Twenty-five years later, their story was retold in Hitchcock's celebrated 'ten-take' wonder, *Rope*. Based on Patrick Hamilton's play of the same name, *Rope* starred John Dall and Farley Granger as the two killers, and James Stewart as the school-teacher who uncovers both the body and the means by which a mentor's excitement over Nietzsche can be twisted into 'a cold logical excuse' for premeditated murder.

Described by François Truffaut as a film in which 'two young homosexuals strangle a school friend just for the thrill of it', *Rope* is actually rather shy about disclosing the nature of the two killers' relationship. We know that 'Brandon' and 'Philip' share an apartment. We know that the joint act of killing young 'David Kentley' provided a thrill not unlike the experience of sex ('How did you feel, during it?' Brandon asks at one point, and Philip replies, 'I don't remember feeling much of anything – until his body went limp, and I knew it was over, then I felt tremendously exhilarated'). We know also that neither man has a girlfriend.

But this is really all we do know. We don't know for certain whether Brandon and Philip share the same bedroom, or whether there are actually two separate bedrooms in the apartment. We don't know for certain whether or not Philip has ever had a girlfriend, though we are told that Brandon has. *Rope* is a film about detection, in which no 'evidence' of sexual deviance is fully corroborated. In the film's final scene, when James Stewart's character exclaims in horror, 'I don't know what you are', we are inclined to share in his frustration. Reduced to nuance and connotation, neither confirmed nor categorically denied (since a denial only arouses further speculation), the homosexuality of our two beautiful murderers was all but erased from a film marketed on the claim that it contained few cuts.

In 1959, the case was re-opened. Richard Fleischer's *Compulsion* starred Dean Stockwell as 'Judd' and Bradford Dillman as 'Arty' in a version of the Leopold–Loeb story that came marginally closer to the truth. Fleischer's film followed the killers to court, bringing in Orson Welles as Clarence Darrow, the defence attorney who delivered them from the death penalty but conferred the taint of pathology on generations of gay men thereafter.

Still the film manages to avoid mentioning even once the homosexual relationship that existed between the two men. We know that Judd is regarded by his schoolfriends as 'sad', and that he likes to 'take orders' from Arty, who is variously described as 'funny', 'brilliant' and 'the nervous type'. The nearest we get to an open acknowledgement of homosexuality is when the prosecuting attorney condemns the two killers as 'immature boys of diseased minds'. But even this euphemistic allegation has to be weighed up against the film's 'evidence' of Arty's interest in girls.

Some people might argue that it would have been better for everyone if homosexuality had been struck from the record altogether. Others might feel compelled to remark that the history of queers and film is a catalogue of such crimes and misdemeanours.

Tom Kalin grew up in Chicago. His father worked for the National Council on crime and delinquency. His grandmother kept a scrapbook of newspaper cuttings chronicling the case of Leopold and Loeb. 'Even as a kid I was obsessed with them', he recalls. 'I'd see the photographs of these two beautiful boys from the 1920s, and there was something in them that told me they were homosexual. Even before I knew I was gay, there was something about them that fascinated me.' In 1991, Kalin made something of a name for himself on the independent film scene as the director of *They Are Lost to Vision Together*, a superior piece of AIDS agitprop fuelled by his own AIDS activism and shaped by his involvement with New

York's cultural activist collective Gran Fury. On the strength of this dazzling thirteen-minute short, he managed to secure $100,000 to finance his first feature film.

Originally intending to do a remake of the D. W. Griffiths classic *Intolerance* ('involving three narratives about lesbian and gay invisibility, and the way history is distorted'), Kalin eventually decided to focus on just one strand – the story of Leopold and Loeb. Produced by Christine Vachon (producer of Todd Haynes's surprise hit *Poison*), and mixing elegant retro-chic with disturbing anachronistic detail, *Swoon* is as visually unsettling as it is ideologically troubling: a portrait of homo-psycho killers in shades of Bruce Weber and Herbert List. Hardly the kind of film to answer the call for 'positive' images. Hardly the sort of thing you'd expect from a director with Kalin's history.

Asked during an interview to justify his 'representation of homosexuality', Kalin responded by saying that he made the film in order to set the record straight, 'to state publicly, once and for all, in an unabashed and direct fashion, the facts of the case'. In a sense, *Swoon* could be considered a direct response to *Rope*, a rejoinder to the scene where Brandon reveals the body of David to his former mentor. 'Go ahead and look' he shouts at Rupert. 'I hope you like what you see'.

Kalin doesn't ask us to like what we see, merely to understand his reasons for showing us it. Shot in cold black and white (in sharp contrast to the warm hues of home-romances *Maurice* and *Brideshead*) *Swoon* lays the facts of the story bare. On the promise of sexual favours, the sociopathic Richard (Daniel Schlachet) charms the love-struck Nathan (Craig Chester) into kidnapping the son of a rich neighbour. Richard later kills the boy, and they attempt to hide the body, pouring acid over the face and genitals. Led by a pair of reading glasses discovered at the scene of the crime, the police arrest Nathan and bring Richard in for questioning. The boys' fabricated alibi (that they were in the company of two girls on the night of the murder) soon falls apart under examination. Richard attempts to pin the murder on his partner, who in turn confesses all but the actual killing.

For the first half of the film, Kalin invites us to identify with Nathan – his naive equation of glamour with deviance, his amoral view of criminal behaviour as little more than a means to alleviate the pain of obscurity and guarantee his place in the history books. 'Killing Bobby Franks together will join Richard and I [*sic*] for life', he claims at one point. And when he reels off a list of famous homosexuals (Wilde, Forster, Frederick the Great), we are left in no doubt that he longs to hear his own name uttered in such distinguished company.

But *Swoon* isn't all whimsy. Kalin cleverly underlines (and undermines) the uses of official history with newsreels recalling the hysteria that surrounded the case. A crackling voice over tells us that, following the discovery of the body, 'at Harvard School for Boys, bachelor schoolmasters were taken in for questioning'. The use of archive footage serves another purpose too. By carefully setting the actions of Leopold and Loeb in a social context of violence and prohibition, Kalin implies that they were, to some extent at least, products of their time.

Such distancing does have its drawbacks, however. By the time the case comes to court, and the director totally abandons subjective story telling in favour of a didactic filtering of the crime through the various homophobic institutions of the state (culminating in a delightfully absurd scene where Nathan and Richard cuddle on a bed surrounded by a team of quack psychologists and phrenologists), we have almost forgotten what it was that they were put on trial for. That the prosecuting attorney seems more interested in proving sexual abuse of the boy than in the fact of his murder is of no small importance. Indeed, it corresponds rather neatly to the fact that Kalin himself is more interested in the sexuality of his two antiheroes than in the appalling nature of their actions. Described as the film which 'puts the home back into homicide', *Swoon* is also a film which takes the mess out of murder.

That *Swoon* shys from showing us the awful truth of the killing is both the root of its strength and its greatest weakness. By concentrating his attention on the mythologies surrounding the case, Kalin presents a forceful argument for the process by which internalized homophobia can result in criminality. 'I wanted to murder the idea of suffering as my condition', Nathan complains at one point, and the film shows us how he did it: by passing the suffering on to somebody else. By failing to illuminate the exact nature of that suffering, Kalin risks being charged with an erasure of truth no different in kind from that which his film stands as such a strong denouncement of.

Perhaps that's the price you pay for retaining some sense of duty to the cause. The true horror of murder, after all, is hardly something the movement would like to have to stomach, hardly something 'People Like Me' would wish to be associated with. Still *Swoon* is a landmark film. Depending on your perspective, it either rewrites history or puts history to right. Either way, it takes the history of queers, film and protest into another era. There is no going back now.

End of the Road

REMEMBER *Badlands*? *A Bout de Souffle*? *Butch Cassidy and the Sundance Kid*? *Bonnie and Clyde*? Gregg Araki does. His third feature, *The Living End*, borrows the formula for every couple-on-the-run film you've ever seen and, well, runs with it. The only difference is, the outlaws on the road through Araki's existential universe are both gay. And cute. And HIV positive. And this is not a tribute, or a spoof, or a rip-off. It's 'historical revisionism'. It's 'New Queer Cinema'. And it's cool, okay?

The critical term 'New Queer Cinema' was the invention of *Village Voice* critic B. Ruby Rich. Overexcited by the number of gay and (to a lesser extent) lesbian films she saw on the festival circuit during the year 1991–2, Rich trumpeted the arrival of what she claimed was a new kind of gay cinema. A cinema packed full of fun and the desire to make trouble. A cinema less interested in boring old humanist approaches to gay art than in the alleged hipness of modern gay experience. A cinema more confident than any that had gone before – sexier, stronger, faster.

According to Rich, the 'Queer New Wave' originated in Toronto and reached critical mass in *Sundance*, before hitting festivals in Berlin, Amsterdam and New York. Jarman's *Edward II*, Todd Haynes's *Poison* and Tom Kalin's *Swoon* were all part of it. So too was *The Living End*. Four films without a common vocabulary, strategy or political concern, all claimed as part of the same impulse. Why? Because what they share is 'style' Why? Because they're all 'irreverent', 'energetic' and 'full of pleasure'. Why don't I buy it? Because much the same could be said about the films of David Lynch, if you happen to take pleasure from seeing women having the shit kicked out of them, and I've yet to hear anyone claiming him as Queer.

Of course it isn't the claiming that counts so much as what is affirmed at the box office. As a marketing strategy, the prefixes 'New' and 'Queer' were supposed to communicate the idea that these films were hot tickets. Only that isn't quite how things turned out. By the time *Swoon* reached London in September 1992, the 'New Queer Cinema' wasn't so much waving as drowning. The Institute of Contemporary Arts hosted a two-day conference with participating film-makers and critics. The advance press coverage was encouraging. The audiences stayed at home.

It wouldn't matter so much if the directors riding the crest of the Queer New Wave continued to deliver the goods once the panel parties were over. Haynes and Kalin both did, and will do again. The problem with Araki is that, despite his obvious passion for the art and graft of film-making, his results are a bit of a mess. If this is less true of *The Living End* than of his previous two films, it's true none the less. Taking the 'Queer As Fuck' posturing of queer activism at face value, Araki shakes up a cartoon cocktail of sex and violence that occasionally hits the right nerve but lacks any real conceptual clout. It's a hangover from punk, which came rather late to Los Angeles, and Araki is a damned sight more comfortable with it than he can afford to be.

The Living End is the story of Jon, a cute young film critic who listens to too many Smiths records, and Luke, a cute young drifter with a pistol in his pocket and a whole load of Echo and the Bunnymen lyrics in his head (or maybe it just seems that way, maybe the youth of Los Angeles actually talk like that). Thrown into an unlikely liaison when Luke inadvertently shoots a cop, the two set off on the bitter-sweet, brave America trail, shooting and shagging as they go.

At least the sex between the men is hot. Despite the film's claim to being mad, bad and dangerous to show, the remainder of the script is just too cool for discomfort. Araki reckons the film 'came from a very dark, personal place – those feelings of dread and insecurity which characterized the mid-late 1980s AIDS crisis which pervaded the consciousness of my whole generation'. Personally, I find it hard to believe that this couple of anti-heroes' antibody status is of any greater consequence than the fact that they wear stressed leather jackets. In the self-consciously hip world these dudes inhabit, it's just another symptom of strung-out Californian cool – that strange affliction that makes you squint when you speak, say 'fuck' a lot, fill your apartment with giant inflatable dinosaurs and your windscreen with plastic icons. Like the man said, 'Hey, I can drive!'

Struggling to get a look-in on the margins of such a hard-driven boy-chick fantasy, women figure in one of two ways. Either they're emotionally dependent fag-hags (Jon's friend Darcy, whose entire life revolves around waiting for his call), or inept serial killers (the dykes who try to dispatch Luke at the start but end up watching him drive off in their car. Think about it – at least Sharon Stone got her man). Araki has made a few spirited attempts to defend himself against charges of misogyny ('Some of my best friends are women', and so on). The plain truth of the matter is that he's just too chilled out by his own iconoclasm to let a little thing like sexual politics stand in the way.

Whereas Haynes and Kalin each offered a complex critique of the queer transgressions they celebrated, Araki offers none, banking instead on his in-your-face posturing to blind us to his intellectual and political shortcomings. At one point, one of his characters asks the question 'Where do we go from here?' Where indeed? With *The Living End*, the 'New Queer Cinema' truly reached the end of the road. 'Historical revisionism' my eye. We may be dealing with a pair of characters called Jon and Luke, but Godard never really enters the frame. Forget *Badlands* too. Just think *Thelma and Louise*, with dick for brains.

Genre Bender

THERE is a moment in Pedro Almodóvar's film *Law of Desire* where Carmen Maura (playing the part of Tina, a transsexual and would-be actress) exchanges a long, longing look with real-life transsexual and actress Bibi Andersen (playing a biological woman). In a wilfully improbable set-up, Maura is on stage performing the closing scene from Cocteau's *The Human Voice*; Andersen is waiting in the wings. The only words spoken are those scripted by Cocteau. The unspoken desires are communicated through Tina's poor grasp of the character she is playing and her outrageously improbable acting style.

It's a wonderful moment, in which the performance of love and gender relations is taken to its logical extreme; a moment queerer by far than the film's infamous opening scene, in which a pretty young man offers his arse to the camera and moans 'Fuck me'. Shortly after the 'performance', Tina's gay brother Pablo (the director of the play) accuses her of 'over-acting'. As every lesbian or gay viewer ought to know, this isn't the half of it.

Law of Desire (1987) is the most overtly gay of all Almodóvar's films, by which I mean that the plot revolves around a homosexual couple (Pablo and his jealous lover Antonio, played by the fag's favourite, Antonio Banderas). Almodóvar himself has always maintained that he hates 'obvious homosexual expressions', even going so far as to suggest that the homosexual relationship in *Law of Desire* could just as easily have been a heterosexual one (an interesting idea, given that some feminist reviewers of his 1989 offering *Tie Me Up! Tie Me Down!* took exception to what they interpreted as a gay sadomasochistic fantasy enacted by a heterosexual couple).

Less persuasive is the director's insistence that there is no evidence of a queer sensibility in his films. Of course Almodóvar wouldn't be the first homosexual artist to play down his identity for the sake of a wider audience. But as Paul Julian Smith points out in his stimulating book *Laws of Desire: Questions of Homosexuality in Spanish Writing and Film, 1960–1990*, there is a tendency for such denials to be used in collusion with those who would deny homosexuality any cultural specificity. Certainly, the disavowal of homosexual themes has long been a part of many straight critics' strategy for dealing with Almodóvar. Either they are regarded as being marginal to the film in question, or (as in the case of the lesbian relationship at the heart of his first feature, *Pepi, Luci, Bom and the Other Girls on the Heap*, 1981) they are ignored altogether. And of course the man himself hasn't gone out of his way to draw anyone's attention to the oversight.

Reviewing *Law of Desire* for the *Guardian* in 1987, David Leavitt defended Almodóvar against gay critics who were accusing him of a closet mentality, pointing out that, like the director himself, his characters existed in an enclosed world where homosexuality is simply not an issue. This may be true, but it would be wrong to conclude therefore that Almodóvar is somehow concerned with promoting the 'naturalness' of homosexuality. While some lesbian and gay film-makers struggle (usually unsuccessfully) to provide us with so-called 'positive images', Almodóvar flips us a selection of queer characters who are invariably mad, bad or dangerous to know. Rather than offending our sensibilities with their demented, often murderous actions, they provide us with a reminder that 'gay' needn't be 'good' to be interesting.

Not that 'gay' as a measure of self-identification necessarily comes into it. One of the most interesting aspects of Almodóvar's work as a 'gay' director is his rejection of fixed positioning and earnest politicking in favour of a celebration of the 'unnaturalness' and fluidity of all sexuality. In *Pepi, Luci, Bom* . . . a lesbian punk singer urinates over a policeman's wife and bingo – Luci's in love! In *Labyrinth of Passion* (1982), the disguised son of an emperor lives out his sexual fantasies in a trash cocktail of mistaken identities, gender confusion and genetic engineering. In *Law of Desire*, Antonio makes the transition from defensive heterosexual to obsessive homosexual in under twenty-four hours. In the weird and wonderful world of Almodóvar, nothing is determined – not even the conventions of the genre, which can mutate at the fluttering of an eyelash (usually false).

In spite of the director's protestations, I would argue that there is something undeniably queer about Almodóvar's disrespect for generic convention. Variously described as melodramas, farces, black comedies or social satires, his films all share a playful disregard for the rules of the game. Moods swing, plots switch gear – all in the time it takes for a woman to beat her husband to death with a ham bone (*What Have I Done to Deserve This?*, 1984), or a man called Angel to confess to the rape of one woman and murder of four men with a hairpin (*Matador*).

Almodóvar's films are not simply 'non-realist'; they are positively 'anti-realist'. His characters inhabit a world which regularly draws attention to its own construction, often via the old film-within-a-film technique (employed in *Pepi, Luci, Bom ...* , *Labyrinth* and *Law of Desire*). And on those rare occasions when the camera doesn't give the game away, the characters themselves do.

Towards the end of *Law of Desire*, Tina is alone in her apartment with Antonio. What she doesn't know is that Antonio (who at this late stage in the game is acting straight again) has just murdered Pablo's previous lover in a fit of jealousy. Pablo phones to warn her, stressing that she should 'just act natural'. But what on earth does he mean by 'natural'?

Life's a Drag

BERNADETTE, alias Terence Stamp, has her mind on her driving, her hands on the wheel and her mascara'd eye on the road ahead. Sitting in the back seat are her two travelling companions, Mitzi (Hugo Weaving) and Felicia (Guy Pearce), dolled up to the nines and intent on having fun.

Bernadette is having none of it. Brushing a stray hair back from her face, she informs her friends that she has no intention of joining in their frolics, at least not before they agree to drop the subject of wigs, penises, dresses, bust sizes and 'bloody Abba'.

Just to my left, squatting in the aisle, a seven-foot, silver-clad drag queen called Sassy Stryker is laughing so hard her wig has fallen off. Or perhaps she wasn't wearing one. Sassy was one of the late arrivals; in the dim light of the preview theatre, it's hard to tell what her own special creation is.

The Adventures of Priscilla, Queen of the Desert, released 1994, is a road movie with a difference. It tells the story of a trio of Sydney show girls – two drag queens and a transsexual – busing it across the outback to fulfil a four-week cabaret booking at Alice Springs. It is a film in which hope springs eternal, in which no problem is insurmountable just so long as you're equipped with a handful of bitchy one-liners and a trunk full of gorgeous gowns.

And this is certainly a screening with a difference. Invitations were extended to a cross-section of London's drag demi-monde, requesting the pleasure of their company and the wisdom of their insight. Based on the numbers who'd promised they would definitely be there no matter what, and allowing for a few snapped heels and mislaid eyelashes, the promoters have catered for twenty, which is about the maximum the cinema can hold.

Shortly before I left the house, housewife superstar Lily Savage phoned to say that she was really sorry and all that, but she wouldn't be able to make it on account of being tied up with some telly people. 'What's it all about anyway?', she rasped. I explained that, basically, the idea was to round up a bunch of drag queens, stuff them full of food and drink, sit them in front of a film about another bunch of drag queens, and record their responses. Lily laughed. 'Rather you than me', she said, then rang off.

A few hours later, I was beginning to see what she meant. It was 6.30, the invite had said 6, and so far I was faced with four drag queens in full regalia and one pantomime cow in a Goldilocks wig.

First to make an entrance was Portia. Portia is a friend of the director, a native Australian, and a shining example of how to keep a cool head in a crisis – even under a mane of chestnut curls. The trouble started when Transformer – a one-time Alternative Miss World, the one who looks like Rod Hull and Emu fighting their way out of a Victorian flower-seller – decided to walk off with the sandwiches, only to return five minutes later and then disappear into the ladies' to powder her nose (from the inside, if her energy levels thereafter were anything to go by). 'I deliberately wore my biggest hat,' she explained when it was suggested that she should either remove it or sit nearer the back, 'so that nobody else would be seen. If you'd told me the dimensions of the cinema, I would have made one to fit.'

Next to arrive were Chloe, whose stylishly angled beret and studied posture suggested years of poring over pictures of Lauren Bacall, and 'Miss' Winston, who is a dead-ringer for 'Miss' Naomi Campbell, only a shade more beautiful. By the time the cow came crashing down the stairs, riding roughshod over a trail of bread triangles and fancy sandwich fillings, the photographer was starting to fret about photo opportunities, and I was starting to fret about the projectionist, who was looking less than happy.

And then the lights went down. Someone asked for popcorn, and received a sharp clip across the ear-ring. Half an hour into the film, the cow's head had fallen in the aisle, the drag queen quota had risen to seven, and everyone appeared to be having a gay old time. They shrieked when Felicia, taking her turn at the wheel, suddenly jammed her foot on the brake, causing Bernadette to jam her lippy up her nose. They hollered when Bernadette rescued Felicia from a queerbasher intent on raping her, confirming with two solid punches that a trannie-fucker is no match for a trannie who refuses to be fucked with. They applauded when our three heroines were upstaged by a woman with a rare gift for propelling ping-pong balls from her lower portions. They fell strangely silent when someone asked Felicia what she and her friends did for a living and she replied, 'We dress up in ladies' clothes and dance around miming to other people's songs.'

By the time the lights come up, Sassy Stryker has her yellow cloud of a wig on, Portia has her kit off, and most people seem to agree that *The Adventures of Priscilla, Queen of the Desert* is 'absolutely fabulous', if not better. 'Simply divine!' coos Chloe, as she bolts for the door. 'Loved every minute. I'd recommend it to anybody.'

'Fantastic!' agrees Winston. 'I don't see why it should be a 15. It should be a PG, then everyone could learn from it. Whenever I meet children, they're fine. Adults are the ones who poison kids' minds, then you get kids growing up with all these silly adult prejudices.'

'Fabulous!' enthuses Sassy. 'Very different, very colourful, very vibrant. I think it might have been even better with gay actors, but that's a very gayist point of view, isn't it?'

'Loved it!' say Sandra and Lucia, two of the late arrivals. Sandra's favourite bits were 'the costumes, the scenery and the storyline'. Lucia's favourite bits were all attached to Guy Pearce. 'My husband will kill me for saying this, but Guy Pearce has got everything I look for in a man. He's got the most divine body, the most fabulous tush, and he looks fierce in drag!'

'Wonderful!' sighs Portia, slipping into a pair of jeans and a T-shirt. 'It's so Australian, it makes me homesick. The drag-talk is all very Sydney. And I miss all those costumes. They don't really do it like that here, do they? Here it's all pretty drag, not freak drag. Although . . . '

She nods in the direction of Transformer, who appears to have calmed down rather a lot since the film began. 'It made me cry', Transformer confides. 'I thought it was very moving. The problem is, it makes life seem a bit too easy, doesn't it? I wish my life were that fucking easy. I mean, the film is nice. It gives you a sense of euphoria or whatever, but so does Ecstasy. When you come down, you realize that life isn't quite like that.'

Over in the corner, Portia, Sandra and Lucia are discussing the arrangements for next week's gig. 'They don't have a cassette player there,' Portia is saying, 'so we'll have to get hold of that track on vinyl.' The others are deciding on a place to go to eat. 'We'll have to go together', someone speaks up. 'Safety in numbers, girls.'

Transformer exits and totters off, alone, to the nearest tube. On the way, she is harassed by a man shouting that people like her 'belong in a bloody zoo'. Where is a trannie with a solid left hook when you need one?

Cruising the Vampire

'UNLIKE so many movie stars,' Boyd McDonald once wrote, 'Robert Ryan was able to portray a real heterosexual.' McDonald's assessment of Ryan's acting ability was part of a review of *Clash by Night*, included in his entertaining book of queer film criticism, *Cruising the Movies*.

It would be interesting to know what the same author makes of Tom Cruise. Unlike so many movie stars, Cruise seems to have no trouble at all playing queer-coded characters, but is unable to portray a 'real homosexual'. The extent of his handicap was first hinted at when it was announced that he was to play the vampire Lestat in Neil Jordan's film adaptation of Anne Rice's cult novel, *Interview with the Vampire*, released in Britain in 1995.

Back in the 1970s, *Interview with the Vampire* was required reading among gay men, who got off on the novel's graphic descriptions of homosexual sex, as related by the reluctant vampire Louis to the nervous journalist conducting the 'interview'. 'He was pressing the length of his body against me now,' Louis confesses at one point, 'and I felt the hard strength of his sex beneath his clothes, pressing against my leg . . . '

Having accepted the role of Lestat, Tom Cruise ought rightly to have been the one doing all the pressing. Only, from the moment he was cast, rumours spread that he had insisted that the book's overtly homosexual elements be excised from the script. Quite why a confirmed heterosexual like Cruise should be prepared to take part in some heavy bloodsucking but shy away from a bit of harmless cocksucking is beyond me. Rice herself (who once admitted to feeling 'like a gay man') seemed to share the popular opinion that Cruise was wrong for the role. 'He's too mom and apple pie', she was quote as saying, around the time the film went into production. 'He should do himself and everyone else a service and withdraw.'

Only he didn't, of course. And judging by the double-page ad she subsequently took out in *Variety*, Anne Rice is glad he didn't. Going back on everything she had said previously, the author enthused wildly about the film in general and Cruise's performance in particular. Most of what she wrote is pretty unrepeatable. Let's just say that the two words 'I loved' cropped up rather a lot.

Of course by the time Rice's ad appeared, most people had their own expectations and were more than willing to share them. Hardly suprisingly, most previews tended to revolve around the homosexual content of the film and the alleged 'queerness' of its star. In an article for the *Guardian*, published before the film was released, Mark Simpson made the salient point that *Vampire*, for all the fuss made over its homoerotic subtext, was simply the latest in a long line of films which have capitalized on Cruise's curiously ambiguous screen appeal. What marked out *Vampire* as different from previous Cruise vehicles, he insisted, was that it was derived from an overtly homosexual source and that Cruise was playing a character who, if not exactly homosexual, was certainly polymorphously perverse.

So what of the film itself? A week before *Vampire* opened in Britain, an article in *The Independent on Sunday* described it as 'the most candidly gay movie to come out of mainstream Hollywood'. One suspects that the writer was simply trying to draw attention to himself – his claim is utter nonsense. If by 'gay movie' we mean a film which acknowledges and plays to a gay audience, then *Vampire* is no more 'gay' than Neil Jordan's previous exercise in sexual tourism *The Crying Game* (show me a gay man who didn't twig straight away that the soldier's 'girl' was a man in drag and I'll show you a homosexual who doesn't get out enough). Whatever the truth behind the rumours about Cruise cutting up the script (he denies them completely), the finished film is not only lacking in anything that could aptly be described as gay sex or sensibility – it's not even remotely erotic.

The release of *Vampire* in Britain happened to coincide with the publication of *A Queer Romance* – a collection of essays on lesbians, gay men and popular culture which I had a hand in editing. In it, I made a case for *Top Gun* as a queer film, on the basis that what is denied at the level of narrative (i.e., homosexuality) can be deciphered through inspection of the textual codes (i.e., homoerotic spectacle, male bonding rituals, testosterone-fuelled aerial acrobatics and the total implausiblity of Cruise's on-screen romance with Kelly McGillis).

The ironic thing about *Vampire* is that it presents us with what is very clearly a homosexual narrative, then goes to every effort to deny it. Two men (Lestat and Louis) meet in an orgy of bloodlust, before settling down into a pretended family relationship, complete with an adopted child (Claudia) and the usual rows over infidelity and good housekeeping. Still everything is heavily coded as straight, right down to Cruise's exaggerated impersonation of a queen bitch. His performance is certainly camp, but it's the brand of camp favoured by 'upmarket' female impersonators and downmarket male game-show hosts – the kind that draws attention away from homosexuality, not towards it.

Vampire probably qualifies as a 'queer' film, purely on the grounds that any film about a bunch of orally fixated bloodsuckers is bound to open itself to a queer reading. But it's not nearly as queer as it ought to be, considering its star's track record and the potential of its narrative framework. If the debate over outing is to impact on the film at all, then it ought really to be outed as a straight film that wants to have its bite of the queer cake and eat it too.

What more can I say? I cruised the movie – it didn't cruise me back. Oh well, he was far cuter in *Top Gun* anyway.

Part five

Symptoms

Dying Young

'DYING', in the immortal words of Sylvia Plath, 'is an art, like everything else.' And she ought to have known, better than anybody. As she boasted in 'Lady Lazarus',

I do it exceptionally well.

I do it so it feels like hell.
I do it so it feels real.
I guess you could say I've a call.

That call came from her agent, I'll bet. I can just hear the sales pitch. 'Do it soon, while you're still young! Do it now, while you're still famous! Do it dramatically, and we'll double the sales on your next volume!' In those days, a broken life could still run to a few thousand editions.

When I was a teenage white punk – and a complete dope to boot – I used to fantasize about dying young. At thirteen I knew every line of 'Lady Lazarus' off by heart. I particularly liked the bit about rising up out of the ashes with red hair and eating men 'like air'. I never saw a picture of Syliva Plath with her red hair (all the pictures I had of her were in black and white), but I did possess plenty of photos of myself sporting a fiery orange mop – a tribute to Ziggy, who had charted his own rock and roll suicide, and to Johnny Rotten, who had made no bones about the fact that there would be no future for me, the Queen or anybody else listening.

And then along came Blondie, advising everyone old enough to appreciate the advantage of good cheekbones to 'die young, stay pretty', to 'live fast' and 'leave only the best behind'. That certainly struck a chord. Remember this was 1979, two years after they buried Elvis. What self-respecting thirteen-year-old would choose to end up an over-stuffed hamburger when they could be remembered like James Dean? Or even Sid Vicious for that matter?

Funny how you fantasize about the things you think least likely to happen to you. I used to think car crashes were terribly glamorous until I witnessed (in graphic detail) a pile-up on the M4. It would be some consolation to think that AIDS had taken the gloss off dying young. Of course for many of us it has. The shocking banality of seeing someone you love die a slow death hardly inspires you to rush out and produce a pop single – unless of course your name is Prince, you read about it in a magazine, and you think it would be simply funky to allude to it in a tale of gang warfare, crack addicts and other sorry signs of the times.

While the epidemic takes its toll on closed communities of individuals who have had their eyes opened to the appalling reality of dying young without the compensation of staying pretty, the culture at large continues to pursue its romance with all things fatal and attractive. In March 1993, in France, a skinny man died of a big disease with a little name. Scarcely a cult figure when he was still alive, Cyril Collard's death from AIDS turned him into a national icon, moving the bigwigs of the French film industry to honour his savagely autobiographical film, *Savage Nights*, with no less than four Césars, the French equivalent of the Oscars, including 'Best Film' and 'Best First Film' (an odd choice, given that he plainly wasn't going to be making any more).

Set in 1986, *Savage Nights* tells the story of Jean, a thirty-year-old, HIV-positive, fast-living bisexual man who, although he practises safer sex with his male lover Samy (and with the various anonymous men he encounters along the banks of the Seine), has unprotected intercourse with his eighteen-year-old girlfriend, Laura. When he does finally inform Laura of his HIV status, she rejects his suggestion of using condoms, insisting that her love is all she needs to protect her. Later, as possessive affection turns to jealous resentment, she convinces herself that she too has become infected, and phones him day and night, leaving recriminatory messages on his answering machine. Neither the duplicity of Jean's behaviour nor the hysteria of Laura's reaction inspire much in the way of admiration, but that was clearly never Collard's intention. In a film driven by a jagged sense of life on the edge, characters and actions shoot past the camera at a feverish pace, without pause for comment or explanation.

Faced with the charge that *Savage Nights* was likely to communicate the wrong message to a generation of Gallic lovers who really ought to be taking more responsibility for one another, a defiant Collard told an interviewer 'my film is not an advertisement for the Ministry of Health!' Nor does it say very much about political responses to the epidemic, except to leave us with the impression that, in France at any rate, there aren't any.

For all that, *Savage Nights* is a deeply significant film. It boldly explores the complex play of emotions fuelled by love in a time of crisis. It boldly reminds us that whilst AIDS is a public emergency, and one which calls for urgent public action, it is also an emergency which is experienced largely in private, in the context of intimate relationships, between private individuals. As Jean explains to a friend who criticizes him for having put Laura at risk, 'sometimes I'll do anything to forget I'm wasting away'. And as he later tries to explain to Laura, there are times when he finds it hard to comprehend fully that the virus is actually a part of him.

By the time Cyril Collard was honoured at the 1993 César award ceremony, *Savage Nights* had been seen by over two million people in France – a country with a population not much larger than Britain, and an estimated five times the number of cases of HIV. Sadly, such sobering statistics seemed to have had little influence on the way in which Collard's death was recorded. 'A generation plunged into the torment of AIDS loses its last romantic', reported *Paris Match*, while the *Journal du Dimanche* swapped 'romantic' for 'decadent', describing the young film-maker as 'the Dorian Gray of the AIDS years'.

Significantly, Collard's death also inspired comparisons with James Dean, the young casualty against whom all young casualties seem forever fated to be measured. What Collard actually had in common with Dean could be written on the back of a postage stamp.

In life, both were young, strikingly good-looking and (if Kenneth Anger is to be trusted) irrepressibly bisexual. In death, they were about as alike as chalk and Camembert. Unlike Collard, Dean was spared the ravages of illness. The coroner's report confirmed that Dean died within seconds of his car colliding with another vehicle. For him, death came swiftly and, one suspects, with relatively little pain. He truly knew the benefit of living young and dying fast.

For Collard, it was a rather different story. In the flurry of press that followed his death, French health educators argued that moulding the dead film-maker into Dean's graven image could prove a useful means of imparting the safer sex message to the nation's youth. (The assumption being, presumably, that nobody can resist a pretty face, though why anyone should expect a shallow regard for physical beauty to have any significant influence over sexual behaviour is quite beyond my understanding. Where is the evidence that the glorification of Dean's death encouraged American teenagers to drive safely?)

Conversely, the marketing of *Savage Nights* in Britain implied that AIDS, far from being the central theme of Collard's film (and, indeed, of his later life and early death), was little more than a sub-plot. The word 'AIDS' didn't even appear on the poster advertising the film, though the words 'passion', 'rage', 'liberty' and (most tellingly) 'love' did. Judging from this determination to market *Savage Nights* as anything but 'an AIDS movie', it is tempting to conclude that what the beatification of Cyril Collard really amounted to wasn't an attempt to raise public awareness about AIDS at all, but, in some peculiar sense, a plot to erase it from the death record.

Almost the reverse thing happened to River Phoenix, who died seven months after Collard, on the morning of Halloween 1993, from a drug overdose. He was twenty-three – old enough to be castigated as an adult who really ought to have known better, young enough to satisfy the media's craving for titillating tales of troubled youth.

And boy, did they make an example of this one. Phoenix, we were reminded ad nauseum, was a child of the 'permissive' 1960s, the offspring of a couple of 'whacked-out hippies', whose other children went by the ridiculous names of 'Leaf', 'Liberty', 'Rainbow' and 'Summer'. The fact that Phoenix was easily identifiable as a gay icon (most notably for his role as the narcoleptic gay hustler in Gus Van Sant's *My Own Private Idaho*) fed into this sense of his Otherness. Like Collard, he was dubbed 'the James Dean of his generation'. He was also described by more than one obit writer as 'a bit of an old hypocrite', a man in whom the tensions between public image (clean-living, health-conscious) and private reality (he died from a lethal combination of heroin and cocaine) were only exposed post-mortem. And naturally when the time came there was somebody at the end of the phone ready to testify to his appalling 'self-indulgence'. Sounds familiar? It ought to. The way it was described, the death of River Phoenix might just as easily have been a result of AIDS.

She probably never intended it to be read in this way, but there is a sense in which Sylvia Plath's poetic record of her attempted suicides prefigures one of the sorriest signs of our times: the inclination to treat death not as the great leveller it really is but as the great marketing opportunity it might hold. As Plath wrote in 'Lady Lazarus'

> There is a charge
>
> For the eyeing my scars, there is a charge
> For the hearing of my heart –
> It really goes.
>
> And there is a charge, a very large charge,
> For a word or a touch
> Or a bit of blood
>
> Or a piece of my hair or my clothes.

There is a charge, also, for the decision to sell *Savage Nights* as a straightforward love story, and for the press campaign to raise River Phoenix up as the new James Dean. While publicists and editors debate what becomes a legend most, the mundane awful truth of dying young generates the occasional headline on page seven.

Heart of Galas

HALF a century before the flamboyant singer and performance artist Diamanda Galas staged her first 'Plague Mass' for the AIDS community of New York, the French theatre poet Antonin Artaud was dreaming of a different epidemic. Railing against the Realist constraints of logic and reason as 'the chains that bind us in a petrifying imbecility of the mind', Artaud grappled with the concept of a 'Theatre of Cruelty': a theatre more immediate, less rational; a theatre of the heart, not the mind; a theatre he likened to the plague, blazing its way through an audience by a process of intoxication and infection, purging everything in its wake. Popular theatre, he argued, was dying on its feet, crippled by its own polite prescriptiveness. If it was to recover from this paralysed condition, it needed to rediscover its primitive ritual function, to invite delirium through the disorienting effects of violence and spectacle. In short, if the theatre was to survive at all, it had to start living dangerously. True theatre, Artaud insisted, was 'the exercise of a dangerous and terrible act'.

Diamanda Galas is a truly dangerous vocalist. Trained in a wide variety of disciplines, from traditional Greek to gospel by way of free jazz, opera and the avant-garde, she sings from a place painfully close to the heart. Always confrontational, always hinting at violence, always prepared to explore extreme states of consciousness, her early solo projects included a homicidal love-song entitled 'Wild Women With Steak Knives'. That was before AIDS began to take hold and she dedicated herself to the 'embodiment' (in live performance and on record) of the physical and political horrors of the epidemic.

Her own brother died of an AIDS-related illness in 1986, though she has always been at pains to point out that this loss alone didn't determine the direction of her work. Signed to Mute Records, Galas spent the best part of the 1980s developing a three-part epic she called 'Plague Mass'. A mass for the living rather than the dead, 'Plague Mass' turned the passive notion of mourning on its head, turned grief into a violent cry for action. Reworking ancient scriptures to her own irreverential ends, Galas launched a spectacular vocal assault on the pieties of a faith which teaches that people with

AIDS are agents of their own destruction, inverting conventional wisdom by calling on God, the angels or whoever the hell was listening to 'give me sodomy or give me death!'

The church didn't take long to find offence. In 1990, following a performance at the Festival delle Colline, no fewer than forty Italian newspapers rallied together to condemn 'the curse of Galas'. A year later she tried to enter the German Catholic church by the back door with a proposed concert opening with Mozart and closing with her own material – only somebody took the time to do a bit of research and a bunch of her recordings were duly sent to a priest for exorcism. Although she regards her work as liturgical in the strictest sense, Galas didn't lose any sleep over it – with 'Plague Mass' she knew she had succeeded in taking all the fun out of their metaphors.

'My voice was given to me as an instrument of inspiration for my friends', she once said, 'and a tool in the torture and destruction of my enemies.' And it is that voice, with its shocking, remarkable three-and-a-half octave range, that decides how, and to what degree, we respond to her work. Galas can sing as sweetly as an angel, and she can retch sounds from her throat like a person possessed. She can lull you into a false sense of security, and she can hit you like a lumbar puncture. Her work is revered by some, renounced by many, and treated with extreme caution even by those to whom it is dedicated as a demonstration of solidarity. Her performances have been described as terrifying acts of psychological healing, as monstrous displays of cultural terrorism, as just plain terrible. *Wire* magazine voted her 1988 album *You Must be Certain of the Devil* the record 'Most Likely to Rid Your House of Unwanted Guests'.

One imagines Artaud would have sat it out. For while there is a world of difference between the 'plague as metaphor' Artaud envisaged and the realities of the 'plague' Galas commits to record, there is something essentially 'Cruel' in the nature of what she achieves through her vocal performances. 'I developed an extreme technique to ride the outer limits', she has said, but it could just as easily have been Artaud talking. To speak, as he did, of 'the anguished, catastrophic times we live in' may carry altogether different connotations today; speaking 'in tongues' with the aid of multiple microphones, Galas has developed a style of vocal delivery that owes far more to a dead poet's idea of 'affective athleticism' and emphasis on ritualistic incantation than to any contemporary notions about shaping a successful musical career. Pop music, she once argued, was purely descriptive – hers was the bloody embodiment of the plague.

To describe a Galas performance is, in a sense, to betray it, but it's a critic's duty to try. In May 1992, Galas performed a short extract from 'Plague Mass' as part of her 'Judgement Day' concert at London's Royal Festival Hall. Stripped to the waist, drenched in fake blood, looking for all the world like an extra from *The Evil Dead*, she contorted her way through half an hour of vocal gymnastics in a rare, raw performance that amply demonstrated her case against 'mourning towards passivity' and left the front seven rows of the stalls reeling from shock, horror or possible ear-damage. 'Were you a witness?' she hissed, her accusation of culpability echoing around the packed auditorium. 'Were you a witness? And on that holy day, and on that bloody day. There are no more tickets to the funeral. The funeral is crowded.'

It wasn't only the words that provoked discomfort. To hear her voice on record is one thing – after all, we're familiar enough with dramatic vocal effects, familiar enough to know not to trust them. To hear her sing live, and witness that voice emanating out of such a tiny frame, is a different experience entirely – one that forces all kinds of emotions up in the listener, from the sheer thrill at her technical accomplishment to the pain of knowing what raw materials went to produce some of those bloody notes.

The 'Judgement Day' concert was part of a promotional tour for her 1992 album *The Singer*. A hymnal of gospel and blues classics, *The Singer* remains by far the most commercial thing Galas has produced to date. Recorded live, stripped to the bare essentials of crashing piano arrangements and robust, swooping vocals, the album sounds as though it were produced simply to demonstrate once and for all that here was one lady who could sing the blues with the best of them. And she does. From the mourning glories of 'Gloomy Sunday' to the crazed celebration of 'I Put A Spell On You', Galas weaves her peculiar dark magic into the familiar pace and patterns of the genre. But these are no straight cover versions. Still there is that extraordinary voice of hers, wrapping itself around the traditional songs of slavery and oppression, subtly altering the meanings, turning the 'balm' in 'Balm In Gilead' to drug therapy, the judgement in 'Reap What You Sow' to a condemnation of impassivity. Galas dedicates her interpretation of the blues to 'the saints of New York City, both the living and the dead', and something in her tortured delivery makes the songs sound as though they are, and have always been, hers alone.

In September 1993, Galas released what is arguably her most heart-rending testament yet. 'Vena Cava' features the singer returning once more to her raging obsessions – only the tone has changed. Originally conceived as an integral part of 'Plague Mass', the piece has aquired a pace and a pitch all of its own – less dramatic, less declamatory. Galas likens it to 'taking hold of a microphone and obscenely amplifying someone's thoughts'. So while gospel songs and electronic drones echo in the background, it is her babbling voice that occupies the fore, more quietly introspective than on anything she has recorded previously.

The title refers to the body's main artery, the one responsible for returning blood to the heart. The theme is the relationship between AIDS dementia and acute clinical depression. The drama hinges on the moment when things slow down and despair begins to set in. Galas takes us into the mind of someone very close to death, invites us to take a look around, to witness the isolation, the anguish, the fragmenting sense of self. Struggling to hold on to something, her protagonist repeats familiar catch-phrases, talks back to the TV, demands 'no secrets, no needles, no punctures', pleads for love and remembrance. When the moment of departure comes, it is to a distorted rendition of 'Silent Night'.

Like 'Plague Mass', 'Vena Cava' is best understood as the record of a live performance. Like 'Plague Mass' it is demanding, harrowing, painful to take in, hard to turn away from. Like all of Galas's best work, it represents an attempt to take us beyond sympathy to compassion in the strictest sense of actually being there, sharing in the torment. The sleeve notes contain a quote from Elaine Scarry, author of *The Body In Pain*: 'to have great pain is to have certainty; to hear that another person has pain is to have doubt'. In these anguished, catastrophic times, the music of Diamanda Galas takes us straight to the heart, straight to where the hurt is. Artaud would certainly have applauded her for that.

Sound and Vision

IN February 1977 – around the time Derek Jarman's first feature film, *Sebastiane*, began scandalizing art-house audiences across Great Britain – David Bowie released the first single from his controversial *Low* album. Unusually for Bowie, 'Sound And Vision' was a song of few words, a taster for an album in which expository lyrics were all but abandoned in favour of opaque instrumentals (or, as he and his collaborator Brian Eno preferred to call them, 'textures'). Interviewed around the time of the album's release, Bowie explained the near absence of lyrics on *Low* by pointing out that he really had very little to say.

Certainly, 'Sound and Vision', with its cold, synthetic rhythms and numb, repetitive vocals, sounds like a man in the final stages of cutting himself off from the world. Bowie's voice isn't even heard until two-thirds of the way through the song's three minutes. 'Don't you wonder sometimes', he croons, 'about sound and vision?' After two minutes of abstract sound, it's the vision he focuses on: 'blue, blue, electric blue', the colour of the room where he will live, alone, with the 'pale blinds' drawn all day and nothing to read ('nothing to say'). For Bowie, who was hitting what he later described as 'an all time low', blue was the colour of physical isolation, of emotional withdrawal, of shutting it all down.

Coming from a film director with a well-earned reputation for creating arresting visual images, Derek Jarman's *Blue* (1993) is a far greater shock to the system than any Bowie could have contrived. A film practically devoid of images, it comprises seventy-six minutes of soundtrack, played against an unaltering blue screen. The sounds (sections of music, snippets of poetry, extracts from diaries) are provided by Jarman's long-term collaborator Simon Fisher Turner. The visions are Jarman's own. Blue was the colour that exploded into Jarman's eyes when he was administered drops for a viral infection commonly known as CMV – a symptom of AIDS that left him almost completely blind. In one sense, the film is a record of Jarman's descent into blindness, of the isolation brought about by the loss of his sight, of his near-confinement to one room, of his body's slow but steady 'shutting down'.

But Derek Jarman isn't David Bowie, and there's no mention here of drawing the pale blinds. Withdrawal – either emotional or physical – has never been part of Jarman's strategy for coping with life's lows. Appropriately, his vision of blue leaves little room for self-pity. 'In the pandemonium of image', his detached voice sounds at the start, 'I present you with the universal Blue.' Already we've moved from the purely personal to the universal. It's a measure of Jarman's courage that, despite his blindness, he can still see the colour blue as offering (in the optimistic words of the film) 'infinite possibility'. This is a far cry from the image of the emotionally numb Bowie, sat staring at his electric blue walls, silently contemplating his isolation, unable (or unwilling) to communicate with the outside world. *Blue* may be a film in which accepted methods of communication are cut off, but it's still one in which the desire to communicate is paramount. Jarman may be trapped in his room, or stuck in a hospital bed, but he still has plenty to say – about AIDS, about death, about grief, about society's treatment of lesbians and gay men, about the functions of art and cinema.

Of course the starting point for Derek Jarman's *Blue* wasn't a David Bowie song. The production notes for the film talk at great length about the work of French painter Yves Klein, 'Painter of the Void', whose blue monochrome tableaux left a profound impression on the young Jarman during his formative years at the Slade art school. Klein's canvases were the product of what he described as 'a pursuit of the undefinable in painting'. With *Blue*, Jarman pursues what he has previously held to be 'undefinable' in the medium of cinema: the experience of someone living (and dying) with AIDS.

It seems strangely fitting, therefore, that this film should be quite unlike any feature film we've ever seen, let alone any previous attempt to 'film AIDS'. It isn't only images that Jarman has abandoned. In his efforts to bring us as close as possible to the experience of his illness, he finally throws out what he has previously, disparagingly described as 'the fictions of cinema': narrative logic, and a cast of 'sympathetic characters' with whom the audience are somehow expected to identify. To label *Blue* an 'experimental' film is both an understatement and a misleading evaluation of its achievements: an understatement, because out of all of Jarman's 'experiments' with the forms and functions of cinema, this stands as the most obviously 'avant-garde'; misleading, because for all its breaks with formal conventions, *Blue* is the least ambiguous, most direct statement this film director has ever made.

Not that it isn't at times difficult to watch, or to listen to. Much of what Jarman says here is bound to offend, not least his obstreperous assaults on AIDS charities, or his cool, disembodied declaration that 'I shall not win the battle against the virus – in spite of slogans like "Living With AIDS" '. Indeed, the entire film is conditioned by a strong sense that time is running out – not only for Jarman himself but for all of us. Hence the calls to arms, the pleas for aggressive political interventions, the bitter invective that punctuates the fond recollections of friends either dead or dying.

But there are other factors at play – the ironic commentary on AIDS treatment 'options' drawn from his hospital diaries, the hilarious send-up of the canon of political correctness, the calm serenity that characterizes much of the poetry. At one crucial moment, Jarman sounds his audience out with the rhetorical question 'If I lose half my sight, will my vision be halved?' The short-term response is to answer, emphatically, 'No'. The long-term response is to recognize that there's one hell of a lot more to filming the blues than meets the eye.

Doctor Strange Love

'ALL books are unfilmable', a rather defensive David Cronenberg announced during a press conference at the 1992 Berlin Film Festival. 'You cannot make a film of a book. It is an illusion to think that you can actually recreate a book on screen. The only way you could do that would be to film the pages of the book and read them off the screen. So, failing that, the film that I've made is really a meditation on William Burroughs and on the writing of *Naked Lunch*. It is not, in a sense, inside the book, but watching the book being written. What I wanted to do was make something that would be a fusion of my art with the art of William Burroughs. It was as though the two of us had gotten into the telepod in *The Fly* and had come out of the other machine fused together.'

It was a charming, if rather conceited, claim to make. And a disingenuous one. If we are going to start talking intertextuality, then Cronenberg and Burroughs go back a lot further than the year of *The Fly* (1986) – further back, even, than 1981, which was the year the director informed *Omni* magazine of his ambition to film 'the unfilmable'. Since as far back as 1974, when he unleashed a plague of killer sex bugs on the occupants of a high-rise apartment building in his first commercial feature, *Shivers*, Cronenberg has cultivated a strain of biological, often venereal, horror that owes far more to Burroughs's fixation with pestilence and the treacherous flesh than to good and faithful horror film conventions.

In Cronenberg, as in Burroughs, the horror isn't outside, waiting to have a stake driven through its heart or be blasted to bits; it's inside, lurking in the final place of refuge, the body. Physical aberration and mutation are the key elements to a catalogue of body horror classics overrun with blood-sucking parasites, cancerous growths, genetic disorders. And always, at the root of the problem, the threat of dangerous sexuality. It is no accident that Cronenberg first broke into film via the taboo area of soft-core pornography. 'I am being this clinician, this surgeon', he once said of his forays into the seductive world of horror, 'and trying to examine the nature of sexuality.'

Nature isn't always nice, and, more often than not, the sexuality Cronenberg uncovers isn't very pretty. In *Rabid* (1976), a woman (played by ex-porn-star Marilyn Chambers) develops a phallic, blood-sucking syringe in her armpit. In *The Brood* (1979), a vengeful wife exercises her repressed rage in the shape of murderous dwarfs that sprout from tumour-like growths between her thighs. In *Videodrome* (1982), a television executive's sexual anxiety carves out a vagina-like wound in his stomach. In *The Fly*, a scientist's ambitions are thwarted by an experiment which intensifies sexual pleasure but climaxes in a visual orgy of putrefaction. And in *Dead Ringers* (1988), carnal knowledge of a woman with a deformed uterus drives a pair of twin gynaecologists to madness and suicide.

If Cronenberg's is a world of indeterminate anxieties and appalling desires made plastic reality, then it is one that Burroughs dreamt of first. The killer sex bug that devoured its way into the ailing flesh of *Shivers* (only to resurface, in hybrid form, two years later in *Rabid*) is a close relative of the marauding viral disease described by Burroughs, first in *Naked Lunch* (where he warns that 'males who resign themselves up for passive intercourse to infected partners . . . may also nourish a little stranger'), and later in *Cities of the Red Night* (where the occupants of a global sexual underworld are forced to confront 'a real messy love death').

Despite Cronenberg's insistence that *Naked Lunch* ('the movie') should 'make perfect sense to people who know nothing of William Burroughs and nothing of my other films', it is hard to imagine anyone gleaning much sense from its off-Beat composition who hadn't previously been exposed to Burroughs's infamous cut-up technique, or wasn't at least familiar with the hallucinatory narrative sequencing of earlier Cronenberg outings like *Videodrome*.

According to the director, 'Burroughs loves the film. It was understood right from the beginning that we wouldn't collaborate in the normal sense of co-writing. He had no desire to write a screenplay. I talked to him many times in the years before I made the film. What I got from him was a complete understanding of what I was doing with the film. There was no dispute whatsoever. One of the things we spoke about, for example, was sexuality. Not being gay myself, I didn't know what the sexuality of the film would be. I didn't know what my perspective on homosexuality would be. He said "Don't worry about it, you have to make the film out of what you are".'

What Cronenberg is, is a master manipulator of sexual anxieties. It was inevitable, therefore, that his *Naked Lunch* would disappoint gay critics looking for a celebration of homosexuality. Even before the film was released, a journalist from the American gay news magazine *The Advocate* warned against expecting too much from 'the heterosexual Cronenberg'. (Cronenberg responded by pointing out, quite rightly, that 'it wasn't as if there were a dozen directors vying for the rights and they gave it to the heterosexual.') Writing in *Gay Times* (May 1992), Al Weisel took the director to task for allegedly reinforcing 'every straight man's worst nightmare about gay sex', and depriving gay viewers ('who don't often get a chance to see their literature on the screen') of the opportunity of seeing two men kissing.

It is certainly true that the heterosexual narrative drive of Cronenberg's fantasy limits the opportunities for exploring gay passions. But, as he freely acknowledges, his *Naked Lunch* is less an adaptation of Burroughs's novel than a reflection on its major themes and ideas. Set in 1953 (the year *Naked Lunch* was written), the film takes as its starting point a line from the preface to *Queer*, where Burroughs suggests that, had it not been for the shooting of his wife, he would never have become a writer. In Cronenberg's idiosyncratic interpretation, the efforts of Bill Lee, an exterminator, to erase the guilt of having shot his wife are substituted for the novel's original homosexual trajectory.

Fearing the consquences of his homicidal actions, a once happily married heterosexual male projects himself into a fantasy homosexual world (known only as 'Interzone', but very clearly a substitute for Tangier). Hooked on the noxious substance he once used to rid people's homes and offices of bugs, he experiences all manner of paranoid delusions. Convinced that he is some kind of secret agent, and taking orders from a giant insect-typewriter with a talking asshole, he allows himself to be persuaded that 'homosexuality is the best all-round cover an agent ever had', and duly begins to act the fag.

Perhaps predictably in the context of a Cronenberg outing, this grim performance of homosexuality brings its associated horrors. At the bar where Bill meets his boy lover Kiki, a man is seen rolling back his sleeves to reveal arms pocked with lesions. Shortly afterwards, Kiki is brutally torn apart by another, older man as he fucks him. At an earlier point during Bill's bogus journey, our hero is overcome by an 'unspeakable horror' which freezes 'the lymph in my glands'. The 'horror' of which he speaks is simply the knowledge that he is homosexual. However, the visible signs of that fact, underscored by Bill's remark that 'a wise old queen taught me that I had a duty to live and to bear my burden proudly for all to see', seem to suggest a horror that is more specifically 1990s than 1950s.

Cronenberg has always insisted that 'the appeal of horror is beyond politics', that 'you can interpret anything in the light of a particularly dogmatic stance'. In many ways he is right, of course, but this doesn't remove the fact that politically-loaded images of infection and decay are central to his scheme. And given the film's free association of intravenous drug-use with homosexuality, of potentially lethal bug powder with violent acts of buggery (embodied in the image of the bug's ominous, drug-crazed, dirty-talking asshole), it doesn't seem particularly dogmatic to ponder whether the naked anxieties of *Naked Lunch* are a reflection of straight society's secret fascination with gay sex and paranoia over AIDS. Indeed we might ask, as Leo Bersani did in his provocative essay on media constructions of anal sex as self-annihilation: 'Is the rectum a grave?'

Before I'm accused of harbouring an essentialist's bugbear, perhaps I ought to point out that it is the homosexual Burroughs, rather than the heterosexual Cronenberg, whom I would most expect to answer in the affirmative. Burroughs's detailed descriptions of polymorphous perversity have always been designed to shock, to revolt, rather than to titillate. The violent sexual images in his novels testify to their author's prurient disgust for the flesh – a disgust hardly shared by Cronenberg, whose treatment of metaphoric malady, from the pestilence of *Shivers* and *Rapid* to the spectacular body-horror of *The Fly*, demonstrates little by way of moralism.

However gruesomely shocking the special effects he employs (and it is worth noting here that the effects in *Naked Lunch* are far less technically gruesome than they could have been), it has always been clear that Cronenberg positively revels in the potential for mutation. If for Burroughs the sins of the flesh take you straight to hell, for Cronenberg they take you to a place that is neither here nor there – an 'Interzone' where moral judgements, like disbelief, are willingly suspended. For all we might label him a director of horror films, Cronenberg is actually far less interested in physical horror than he is in the capacity physical mutation carries for change, for readjustment to a new set of circumstances neither inherently better nor inherently worse than the prescribed 'natural' condition.

In *Videodrome*, this potential is fulfilled during the inauguration of the all-powerful New Flesh. By far the most instructive example, though, is that of Seth Brundle, the emotionally isolated but sympathetic hero of *The Fly*. Brundle, in many ways, is the archetypal Cronenberg protagonist – an outsider who, though troubled by his own sense of not belonging, gradually learns to embrace his 'difference'. Brundle's initial shock at the deterioration of his body soon gives way to a morbid curiosity. Even as his decrepit human flesh is falling away to reveal the hardened body of an insect, Cronenberg has him say, quietly and with no indication of panic, 'I seem to have contracted a disease with a purpose'.

To suggest that there was some 'purpose' to a disease such as AIDS would be wrong-headed and offensive. To deny any purpose but homophobia in Cronenberg's strange love of the temporal flesh would be just plain foolish.

Seeing the Funny Side

SAY what you like about *Philadelphia* – there weren't many good jokes in it. As much as Hollywood's 'first AIDS movie' made Larry Kramer 'really angry' (what doesn't, these days?), one suspects that its earnest, proselytizing tone struck the right note with his old sparring partner Edmund White, who decreed in 1987 that 'if art is to confront AIDS more honestly than the media have done, it must begin in tact, avoid humour, and end in anger'. For White (who, it has to be said, rarely sees the funny side of anything), 'Humour seems grotesquely inappropriate to the occasion . . . humour suggests that AIDS is just another calamity to befall Mother Camp'.

Whatever the success – or not – of *Philadelphia* (1994) in persuading homophobes to hate us all a little less (or at least those of us who wear smart suits and avoid kissing our boyfriends in public), its resounding commercial achievement suggests that AIDS could be the Next Big Theme to befall Mother Multiplex. After years of lying dormant in some producer's filing cabinet, moves are afoot to turn Kramer's landmark piece of AIDS agit-prop *The Normal Heart* into a film. Other productions under way are Francis Ford Coppola's *Cure*, Joel Schumacher's *Intimate Relations* and film versions of award-winning stage plays *Marvin's Room*, *Jeffrey* and *Angels in America*. In the meantime, we have *And the Band Played On* (1994), an adaptation of Randy Shilts's best-selling volume of AIDS reportage.

Originally made for American television, there is something frankly opportunistic in the way that Roger Spottiswode's star-studded dramatization was rushed out for a British theatrical release hot on the heels of *Philadelphia*. One assumes that the version we have been invited to see has been substantially cut down to size – how else do we account for all the holes in the plot? Still at two and a half hours it runs the risk of being dubbed *And the Band Played On, and On, and On* . . .

The first problem is lack of focus. This is the story of a group of researchers at the Center for Disease Control, led by Dr Don Francis (Matthew Modine), who bravely do battle with a corrupt officialdom which puts profits and political expediency before the interests of public health. It is also the story of the race between American and French scientists to identify the HIV virus and thereby claim their place in the history books. And it is the story of 'Patient Zero', the French-Canadian flight attendant singled out by Shilts as The Man Who Brought AIDS To America.

Added to this, there are all manner of sub-plots: the clashes between 'responsible' gay community leaders such as Bill Kraus (Ian McKellen, typecast again) and the defenders of the gay bath-houses; the refusal of the blood banks to screen blood or trace donors; the reluctance of the media to show interest in a disease perceived to affect only those people (fags, junkies, immigrants) the public generally doesn't like to read about.

With so much going on at once, it is hardly surprising that we never get the chance to develop anything but a passing, casual relationship with the key players. It isn't really McKellen's fault that his big death-bed scene leaves us weeping – with laughter. Which brings me to the main problem with the film as a whole. There are some very funny moments in *And the Band Played On* – though, sadly, one suspects they weren't written in on purpose. Like *Philadelphia*, this is a film which places too much importance on being earnest. Like *Philadelphia*, it is at pains to show everybody in the kindest possible light (including Phil Collins, who makes a brief appearance as the owner of a gay bath-house, prompting this viewer to the conclusion that the casting director missed again). Like *Philadelphia*, this is a film for *them*, by which I mean those lucky people for whom AIDS is not yet a reality.

Two films made very much for us are Richard Glatzer's *Grief* and John Greyson's *Zero Patience* (both 1994). We know they are for us because they dare to be funny about a subject we all joke bitterly about in private, but find it hard to raise a laugh about in public. *Grief* is the story of a gay man called Mark, whose lover died of AIDS one year to the day before the film begins. A script editor on a tacky daytime soap called *The Love Judge*, Mark isn't coping too well with the trials of being stricken with grief and very possibly stricken with love over a straight man named Bill (Alexis Arquette, enchanting as ever). On top of all this, there's the little matter of Mark's larger-than-life boss Jo (played by larger-than-life drag queen Jackie Beat) unexpectedly quitting her job, and his best friend Jeremy harbouring a big secret passion for Bill.

Glatzer based the script for his black comedy on his experience of losing his own lover, and finding it enormously difficult to form emotional or sexual attachments. It is a situation many of us have either been in or observed at close quarters, and it isn't a remotely funny one. Still, *Grief* manages to be outrageously funny in spite of its serious theme, and seriously moving in spite of its outlandish humour. The painful truth of Mark's situation surges through at moments you least expect, strangling the laughter in your throat.

Even more ambitious is *Zero Patience*, in which a flagrant disregard for the pieties evoked by AIDS is matched with a passion for undermining the narrative conventions of Hollywood – in particular the Hollywood musical. The title is an obvious pun on 'Patient Zero'. The plot follows the fortunes of Sir Richard Francis Burton (the notorious Victorian explorer and sexologist, miraculously still young of body in 1993) as he assembles a multimedia museum display on the origins and epidemiology of communicable diseases. Burton's plans are thwarted when he meets and falls in love with the ghost of Zero, back from the dead on a mission to clear his name. George, a local black schoolteacher and close friend of Zero, provides a sobering point of identification as he struggles to make sense of a bewildering range of AIDS treatment options and the competing agendas of doctors and activists. Still, George is no passive victim. Like all the key players in this heavily didactic but curiously engaging drama, he has a song to sing.

Zero Patience is a 'proper musical' in so far as it depends on the mise-en-scène of spectacle and song to communicate what its characters are incapable of saying for themselves. It is also a 'proper' – by which I really mean an honest – AIDS film, though its director displays very little tact and is unwilling, or unable, to avoid humour. The film does end in anger, with the local chapter of ACT UP storming the museum and tearing down Burton's casual representation of the lives they are leading. But even this radical action is an excuse for a show tune.

I don't know what Edmund White would make of all this campery – though I could merit a guess. For me, *Zero Patience* is a laudable demonstration of how deconstructive wit can serve as a weapon, and a timely reminder that laughing in the face of AIDS isn't quite the same thing as treating it lightly. These days, we 'only laugh' when it hurts.

Loving the Alien

'WHEN I was told that I'd contracted this virus, it didn't take me long to realize that I'd contracted a diseased society as well.' These words were written by the late David Wojnarowicz in his acclaimed AIDS memoir, *Close to the Knives*. But they could just as easily have been spoken by Warrant Officer Ellen Ripley in the final reel of *Alien 3*.

Directed by David Fincher (best known for making pop promos for Madonna), the third instalment in the *Alien* saga is not only the most underrated, it is also the most frequently misunderstood. Generally dismissed by the mainstream press (who complained that it lacked the thrills of James Cameron's militaristic *Aliens*), generally ignored by the gay press (who obviously saw it as having no relevance to their readership), it was left to Amy Taubin, writing in *Sight & Sound*, to point out what should have been clear to everyone – that the film was never meant to be viewed as a Hollywood blockbuster; that it is, in fact, an art-house film about the AIDS crisis and the threat to women's reproductive rights.

Looking back, you could argue that the virus was present from the start. Released in 1979, long before AIDS began making news, Ridley Scott's original *Alien* fed off a complex pattern of anxieties around sexuality and the permeability of the body. The creature itself was a Freudian nightmare – a phallus with gnashing teeth and no respect for the distinguishing categories 'masculine' and 'feminine'. In the film's most memorable (and for many people, most appalling) scene, a man is shown 'giving birth' to a baby alien which has been quietly incubating inside his chest.

Cameron's 1986 follow-up succeeded in heightening the drama while simultaneously lowering the stakes. *Aliens* projected the anxieties of the first film into a war zone where they could be far more easily externalized and obliterated. Ripley, the lone human survivor of the first encounter with the hostile alien life form, faces the horror once more – only, as the posters read, 'This time it's war'.

Her motives for risking her life a second time are important. Having spent fifty-seven years floating around in hyperspace, Ripley lands back on earth to learn that her own daughter has died, and that the planet she and her crew touched down on all those years ago is now heavily populated with innocents – 'families', as she says, with a clearer sense of concern than she ever expressed for her original shipmates. Dubious as to the motives of the Company men, but desperate to exorcize a few personal demons (i.e., the nightmare that she is carrying an alien), Ripley agrees to go back into battle.

Supported by a team of marines, she wages war against the nest of marauding aliens and their queen and wins – rescuing a young girl, Newt, and a potential husband, Hicks, from the wreckage. The film ends happily with the three human survivors, plus a friendly android, heading for home in their cosy spacecraft. In the final scene, Ripley tucks the little girl up to sleep, and tells her that it's okay to dream now.

Compared to this comforting militaristic fable, Fincher's film marks the return of the repressed. The difference is clear from the opening credits. While Ripley and her surrogate family sleep soundly, a sequence of sharp edits indicates that something else is moving aboard the ship. A fire breaks out, and the ship is sent hurtling towards the nearest planet – Fiorina 161, a lice-infested, all-male penal colony populated by a motley bunch of shaven-headed sex offenders with English accents and a strange taste in religion ('your basic apocalyptic, millennial, Christian fundamentalism', as one prisoner succinctly puts it). Newt and Hicks are both dead on arrival. Ripley is the sole survivor.

Well, not quite. Bishop, the android who renewed her faith in artificial people in *Aliens*, is still in working order – just. And more importantly, Ripley has brought two stowaways with her. By the time her unconscious body has been retrieved from the wreckage, the first alien has already found a nice warm nesting place inside someone's pet dog. The second alien – a queen – is gestating inside Ripley herself. The nightmare of the second film has become flesh.

Even before this is made apparent, it's clear that body horror is the order of the day. Concerned that Newt's corpse might be harbouring an alien embryo, Ripley requests an autopsy. Her request is met – largely because the prison doctor, Clemons, has already taken a bit of shine to her. The brutality of the film is announced as soon as the little girl's chest is cracked open. 'Would you like to tell me what we're really looking for?' Clemons asks at this point. 'Communicable infection', Ripley replies, reintroducing the disease motif which played throughout the original film.

Before long, she and Clemons have formed a bond which involves a hint of sex and lots of needles. 'What's in that?' she asks, the first time he offers to shoot her up. 'Just a little cocktail', he smiles, reassuringly. The second time she offers her veins to him, he has just confessed that he used to be a morphine addict, and that his addiction led to the deaths of eleven of his patients. 'Do you still trust me with a needle?' he asks. She does. Just as he finishes administering the drug, the first alien appears and rips off his head.

As Amy Taubin commented, 'AIDS is everywhere in the film. It's in the danger surrounding sex and drugs. It's in the metaphor of a deadly organism attacking an all-male community. It's in the iconography of the shaven heads.' It's elsewhere, too. It's in the decision to unleash the alien on a group of sexual degenerates who, having found a new religion, don't have sex any more. ('I've taken a vow of celibacy', one prisoner informs Ripley. 'That also includes women.') It's in the sense of despair which descends on our plucky heroine, the moment she learns from Dillon, the sneering prison leader, that there are no weapons available, no effective 'treatment' for the 'disease'. It's in the desperate attempt to halt the alien's progress in the vein-like channels running throughout the prison basement ('It's a metaphor', Ripley snaps when one prisoner questions her judgement). It's in the director's controversial decision to ignore the lavish sets and shoot almost entirely in close-up, thereby focusing attention on the body as the site of attack.

And most importantly, it's in the body and actions of Ripley herself. Realizing that the Company cares far more for the preservation of the alien than for the welfare of its victims, she urges the prisoners to join forces with her, goading them with the remark: 'They think we're scum and they don't give a fuck about one friend of yours who's died.' Learning that she herself is 'diseased', her first response is to ask one of the prisoners to deliver a swift death. When he refuses (on the grounds that she is more use to him dead than alive), she decides to seek out the alien.

There is something faintly touching about the way she addresses the creature when she (mistakenly) believes that she has finally tracked it down. 'Don't be afraid', she whispers. 'I'm one of the family now.' And there is something profoundly depressing about this, too. For while the development of Ripley's character from the previous film to this one represents a shift away from 'family values' towards an acceptance that we are all 'family' under the skin, it also leaves her no way out but death.

In the film's startling final image, Ripley takes her own life by plummeting backwards into a furnace. The Company men want her baby, and she has no intention of giving it up. As she falls, the alien she is carrying erupts from her body. We see her wrap her arms around it, hugging it closely to her chest. The image is ambiguous – a mixture of grim determination and almost maternal affection.

At the level of horror narrative, Ripley is simply ensuring that the monster dies with her, that it doesn't escape and live on to terrorize other innocent people. At the level of AIDS allegory, you could say that she has come to terms with her fate, that she has learned to love the alien. The question is, what good does her love do her, or any of us?

I Will Survive

WHEN I was a boy I used to scream, shout and dance to disco. Sitting through the opening night West End performance of *Hot Stuff* ('the first 1970s compilation musical', according to co-star David Dale), I didn't scream, I didn't shout and I certainly didn't do the hustle. I left that to the straight couples in matching shell-suits, joyfully reliving their version of the decade that taste forgot – a sort of K-Tel record of crimes against nylon, Lurex and Newton's first law of gravity.

After years of empty speculation, punctuated with far too many Gary Glitter Christmas comeback specials and the occasional 'prophetic' fashion feature in *The Face*, the 1970s revival is finally upon us. And I have to say that, give or take a few fat straight boys in skinny-ribs, it doesn't bear much resemblance to my memories of the decade that shaped my queer consciousness. The songs selected for repackaging under the banner of '1970s classics' are the kind that go with nights down the rugby club, Malibu-and-pineapple and chicken-in-the-basket. Articles in the style press try to persuade us that the 'New Androgyny' of popsters like Pulp's Jarvis Cocker or Suede's Brett Anderson is a meaningful tribute to the days of old. Sorry for scoffing, boys, but someone doing a pale imitation of David Bowie singing-along-a-Smiths record says nothing to me about my life.

Gay men invented the 1970s. Or at the very least they made the decade's finest moments happen. They were behind the scenes when Ziggy had his first moonage daydream in stack heels and lip gloss, and they were out on the dance floor when Grace Jones first sang about needing a man to make her dreams come true. Without gay men there would have been no stardust, no glam drag and no disco. On a slightly duller note, it is also fair to say that without gay men there would have been no Village People. In his 1979 essay 'In Defence of Disco' (*On Record*, ed. Simm Frith and Andrew Goodwin (Routledge, 1990)), Richard Dyer found it hard to defend the 'cock-oriented' look and sound of the faithless five, expressing concerns that 'such phallic forms of disco as Village People should be so gay identified'. I sort of know what he means, but with hindsight I don't find it too hard to forgive them. The Village boys may have come on like Hot Gossip in hard helmets, but they were still a hell of a lot better than Brotherhood of Man.

The straight 1970s gave us wimpy ditties like 'Save All Your Kisses For Me', 'Welcome Home' and 'A Rose Has To Die'. The gay 1970s gave us mighty anthems like 'Do You Wanna Funk?', 'Ain't No Stoppin' Us Now' and 'I Will Survive'. The fact that 1970s disco was essentially an affiliation of black musical tradition with gay club culture has been ably demonstrated by critics such as Dyer and Jon Savage. Indeed, were it not the case that disco was, and continues to be, 'gay music', no one would have got the joke when the Pet Shop Boys sang in 1993 about a man who dances to disco but doesn't like rock. 'Can You Forgive Her?' used disco dancing as a euphemism for closeted homosexuality. That the dancer addressed in the song is made into 'some kind of laughing stock' reminds us also that the association of disco with homosexuality isn't always seen as a positive one. As Walter Hughes recently pointed out (in an essay entitled 'Feeling Mighty Real'), negative critiques of disco tend to echo homophobic accounts of the urban gay male community that emerged during the 1970s: 'disco is "mindless", "repetitive", "synthetic", "technological" and "commercial", just as the men who dance to it with each other are "unnatural", "trivial", "decadent", "artificial" and "indistinguishable" "clones" '. In spite of this hostile construction – or, indeed, perhaps because of it – 1970s disco became 'part of the post-Stonewall project of reconstituting those persons medically designated "homosexuals" as members of a "gay" minority group, and of rendering them visible, individually and collectively'.

Can it really be a coincidence, then, the fact that disco was proclaimed dead at precisely the same time that AIDS began making headlines? And is it really any wonder that 'so many [gay] men' are still inclined to judge disco not on its aesthetic value but on the life and times associated with it? The truth is, disco never really died. Like the community who fostered it, disco outlived the 1980s by developing a series of strategies for its own survival. As the decade progressed, and the lesson that 'silence equals death' was brought home to a generation of dancing queens, disco mutated into a variety of forms – house, garage, techno – each offering a measure of protection against the threat of extinction. Meanwhile, the cover versions harked back to a happier time, to disco's historical and musical roots. The Communards' 1986 cover version of Thelma Houston's 1976 classic 'Don't Leave Me This Way' was both an appeal to a departing lover and a paean to a decade past, a reminder of what that decade symbolized to a community who truly thought they were 'moving together to the promised land'.

In Mark Christopher's short film *The Dead Boys' Club* (1992), a young gay man living in the Age of Anxiety gets a taste of life before the epidemic. Arriving in town for the funeral of his cousin's gay lover, Toby is cruised at the bus-stop by a mean-looking hunk in a vest who scribbles him a note containing a telephone number and the word 'Dick'. Assuming this is some kind of joke, Toby throws the note in the bin and sets off to cousin Packard's house, where Packard and his friend Charles are sorting out the dead man's belongings. Among them are a pair of 'slut shoes' and a stack of Donna Summer albums. 'Your generation will never know what they missed', Charles says when Toby sniffs at the mention of Donna Summer. But he's wrong. Slipping into the dead man's shoes, young Toby finds himself transported back to the heady days of 1970s gay disco while, on the film's soundtrack, Thelma Houston laments the passing of love and time.

Initially freaked out by the unnatural powers of the shoes, Toby decides to put his best foot forward. Stepping out on the street, he is cruised by every passing gay boy. After a close sexual encounter at the gym, he trots along to a club with Packard, condom stuffed in shirt pocket, feet tucked into the shoes for that extra boost of sexual confidence. The club, Packard informs him, 'used to be truly wild'. At the club Toby meets Dick who, it turns out, is a friend of Packard's. Wasting little time on small talk, Toby and Dick go back to Dick's place for what promises to be a night of uncomplicated sex.

In the morning, Toby wakes and, remembering nothing of the night before, is thrown into a panic when he can find no evidence of having used a condom (his is still in his shirt pocket, and Dick's sleeping body is covering the torn condom wrapper). Racing home in his bare feet, Toby runs a bath and, in a scene which parodies today's anxieties about genital hygiene, frantically scrubs his feet to remove all trace and taint of the shoes. When Dick returns the shoes to him, Toby throws them out of the window. They land next to a street-seller, who adds them to his stockpile of second-hand goods. Deciding that he can't live without them, Toby goes looking for the shoes, and meets another boy with similar designs on purchasing a token of the past. The film ends with the two boys smiling shyly at each other over the shoes, and Thelma Houston singing over the credits.

A film which plays with ideas about history, escapism, identity and desire, *The Dead Boys' Club* is both a tribute to that gay old favourite *The Wizard of Oz* and an inversion of 1970s icon Patti Smith's audacious boast, 'well I ain't fucked much with the past, but I've fucked plenty with the future!' Shy Toby hasn't fucked much in the present, but in the course of the film he gets to fuck with the past and thereby overcome his acute fear of sex. If the lesson Dorothy brought back with her from Oz was that there's no place like home, the lesson Toby picks up in *The Dead Boy's Club* is that there's no time like the present – even when the past is only a footstep away.

That it is impossible for today's gay men ever to live fully in the past might seem like rather an obvious statement to make. The same is true for everybody, of course, but it is especially true for a community whose links with the past – embodied in the physical presence of those people who actually lived through that past – are under threat of erasure. Which is precisely why the idea of a past co-existing with the present is such a comforting one, and why the notion of a 1970s revival carries an altogether different meaning for us than simply an excuse to wear silly, colourful clothes.

In the 1990s, it is the fears and frustrations brought about by AIDS, rather than the fashions, which have the greatest bearing on how gay men rework and relive the 1970s. And naturally disco is an integral part of that experience. Declared dead more times than probably any other pop idiom, disco is not only alive and well – it has become part of the language of mourning. In gay clubland the old songs are filling the dancefloors again, rejuvenated and remixed for a generation who measure their pleasure in beats per minute. Songs that were once part of the 1970s gay disco inferno are making us slaves to the rhythm of late nights, bright lights and non-stop ecstatic dancing: 'I Will Survive', 'If I Can't Have You', 'How Deep Is Your Love?', 'Long Train Running', 'Go West', 'Young Hearts Run Free'.

Partly it's a nostalgia trip, of course, a yearning for a return to what many gay men – including some too young to remember – regard as our 'Golden Age'. Only 'love in that time was not as love is nowadays', and inevitably the lyrics carry different meanings now than they did then. Even under the euphoric influence of mood-altering drugs, the sad irony of phrases like 'First I was afraid, I was petrified', 'Don't know why I'm surviving every lonely day', and 'Without love, where would you be now?' can scarcely go unnoted. The nostalgia evoked by lyrics like these is as much nostalgia for life as it is nostalgia for time. Songs that were once sung as records of the agonies of love are now reinscribed with connotation about the agonies of loss.

In that subtle shift of meaning – from romance to mourning – there lies the critical difference between 1970s revivalism and 1970s survivalism. If the renewed hedonism of the 1990s gay club scene is an impassioned form of escapism, it is also one which draws attention to its own cathartic function. For all its promise of complete abandonment, of 'feeling high' and 'sailing away', 1990s gay disco is as much a reminder of the here and now as it is a token of our collective desire to go back to our roots. As Candi Staton sang in 1976 – and again in 1994 – 'Self-preservation is what's really going on today'.